W9-CPF-380

Southern Living GARDEN GUIDE

Garden Projects

Series Editor: Lois Trigg Chaplin

Text by Robert Gandy

Oxmoor House®

Contents

©1998 by Oxmoor House, Inc.
Book Division of Southern Progress Corporation
P.O. Box 2463, Birmingham, Alabama 35201

Southern Living® is a federally registered
trademark of Southern Living, Inc.

All rights reserved. No part of this book may be
reproduced in any form or by any means without
the prior written permission of the publisher,
excepting brief quotations in connection with
reviews written specifically for inclusion in
magazines or newspapers.

Library of Congress Catalog Number: 96-71087
ISBN: 0-8487-2250-7
Manufactured in the United States of America
First Printing 1998

We're Here for You!
We at Oxmoor House are dedicated to serving you
with reliable information that expands your imagination and enriches your life. We welcome your
comments and suggestions. Please write us at:

Oxmoor House, Inc.
Editor, GARDEN PROJECTS Garden Guide
2100 Lakeshore Drive
Birmingham, AL 35209

Editor-in-Chief: Nancy Fitzpatrick Wyatt
Editorial Director, Special Interest Publications:
Ann H. Harvey
Senior Editor, Editorial Services: Olivia Kindig Wells
Art Director: James Boone

Southern Living Garden Guide
GARDEN PROJECTS

Series Editor: Lois Trigg Chaplin
Assistant Editor: Kelly Hooper Troiano
Copy Editor: L. Amanda Owens
Editorial Assistant: Kaye Howard Smith
Garden Editor, *Southern Living*: Linda C. Askey
Indexer: Katharine R. Wiencke
Concept Designer: Eleanor Cameron
Designer: Carol Loria
Illustrator: Kelly Davis
Senior Photographer, *Southern Living*: Van Chaplin
Production Director: Phillip Lee
Associate Production Manager: Vanessa C. Richardson
Production Assistant: Faye Porter Bonner

Our appreciation to the staff of *Southern Living*
magazine for their contributions to this book.

Mailbox

Cover: *Easy Garden Fountain*
Frontispiece: *Painted Pots*

Easy-to-Tackle Topiary

Projects Primer

The fun part of these projects is how you adapt each idea to improve your own surroundings.

All of us want a front yard that welcomes guests, a garden that serves as a retreat, and—perhaps most important—a place to house everything from tools to the family pet. The following pages help you turn these desires into reality. You'll find unusual ideas and practical plans that are easy to accomplish. Best of all, these are, for the most part, weekend projects.

Decorative Arts leads you from your garden to an indoor retreat filled with topiaries, floral arrangements, and festive plant containers. With scarcely more than a glue gun and a paintbrush, you can create lasting bright spots for your home.

While your imagination is your guide when decorating your home, there are right and wrong ways to plant a tree, establish a ground cover, patch your lawn, or transplant valued trees and shrubs. The all-important correct techniques are described in detail in the **Strictly Horticultural** section.

As you leisurely look over your landscape, you will perhaps dream a little about possible enhancements. How about a garden fountain or a small water garden? Once you hear the soft gurgle of water, you may yearn for a bit more color. Nothing is easier than providing a stick or wire trellis for fragrant vines to climb. Or if your tastes run more to the whimsical, turn now to **Garden Decorations** for "pot pals" that add a dash of personality and color to your garden.

Want to change the direction of a walkway, add a brick edging to planting beds, or have a stacked stone wall? **Paving and Masonry** shows you how easy it is to build exactly what you want in the material of your choice.

Hammer and Nails guides you step-by-step through the simplest ways to build a privacy fence, to construct lattice screens, or to create a variety of planters. These improvements do require using woodworking tools but are not beyond the skill level of an average do-it-yourselfer.

You've no doubt discovered the satisfaction of enhancing your own surroundings. So tackle these projects yourself, get a friend to help, modify the instructions, work with prefabricated materials, or even hire all or part of the job out—whatever your preference, you will find in these 34 projects a wide variety of ways to refurbish your landscape.

*Box in a dog-sized spot under your deck; provide a wooden awning to keep it shady. (See **Outdoor Screening** on page 97.)*

Decorative Arts

Gardening constantly sparks inspiration for decorating indoors with the bounty of nature. Sometimes the ideas stem from the beauty of plants—their flowers, leaves, fruits, and seeds. Bringing natural materials inside adds a graceful note. This is especially true in the winter when a lovely dried hydrangea wreath reminds you of summer days in the garden. At other times, problems to be solved bring about creative touches. For example, a search for an accent light might lead to an attractive, alternative use for a clay pot. In this chapter, you will find instructions for eight easy-to-make decorative arts projects that enable you to craft unique accessories and gifts from the garden.

The section on **Moss Containers** offers an easy way to update an old pot with sheet moss from the crafts store. The finished look is fresh, green, and natural—a great transformation from regular potted plant to centerpiece or gift.

In **Topiary Fun**, you will find out how to adapt this classic garden look to produce tabletop accents that can be used for months indoors. Add fruits and flowers to these handsome miniature forms for special occasions.

Because it is so easy to encourage plants to grow around wire forms, ivy is perfect for use in small-scale artistic creations. **Ivy Sculptures** shows you how to train ivy to form living wreaths, globes, ivy trees—or any shape you want.

Dried Hydrangeas are simple to make, but there is an art to the process. You'll learn the secret of cutting hydrangeas at just the right time so that you capture their intense color. Use these large, luxurious blooms to create lovely wreaths, simple flower arrangements, and elegant garlands.

Few decorations are as striking—or as easy to craft and to care for—as a **Living Wreath** made of succulents. Set out on a table, it welcomes visitors in a special way.

Plain clay pots can be painted to serve as charming displays or containers for gift plants, as in **Painted Pots**.

Every gardener who brings plants inside for the winter wants a sunny place to display them. The **Picket-Fence Plant Stand** turns a disorganized corner into a delightful container garden.

Everyday clay pots can also be used to disguise a modern light fixture so that light comes from unexpected sources, as described in **Accent with Lights**.

Cover a wooden crate or box with sheet moss to make a container for houseplants, such as these bromeliads.

Moss Containers

Organize moss-wrapped plants and candles on a tray to create a unique centerpiece.

For a naturally beautiful centerpiece, wrap the pot of a favorite plant in a sheet of moss. Tie the moss in place with raffia.

Moss, considered nature's velvet, can be incorporated into a garden table arrangement, an indoor decorating scheme, or a memorable gift. In a few simple steps, you can transform a plastic nursery bucket, an old clay pot, or a discarded basket into a charming moss-wrapped container that makes a natural backdrop for a plant brought in for the winter. To cover the container, all you need is velvet green sheet moss (available at crafts stores) and glue. The effect can range from rustic to exotic, depending on the shape of the container's base and the finishing details.

For a quick centerpiece, slip a plastic saucer under the nursery pot your plant came in, wrap moss around the pot/saucer combination, and secure the moss with glue. Finish off the look with a raffia ribbon. For a long-lived centerpiece, make a cachepot for the nursery pot by embellishing a separate, slightly larger container with moss. You can remove the plant for watering as needed and then return it to the cachepot. Place a saucer or a plastic liner inside the cachepot to catch any drainage and to protect your tabletop.

Any pot, basket, or wooden box or crate works equally well as a base. Bark, twigs, and raffia wraps can be added to the pot to create interesting shapes or textural contrast.

Getting Started

Look for green sheet moss at a florist's shop or a crafts store or collect fresh moss from your backyard. Remove any chips of bark or clumps of dirt from the moss to improve its appearance and the flexibility of the sheet. If the moss seems dry and brittle, mist its surface with a little water and then let the moss soften a bit before gluing it to the container.

Concentrating on a small area at a time, begin by applying a few dots of glue to the surface of the container. (It is best to work with low-temperature glue to decrease the risk of burning your skin.) Place a piece of moss onto the glue dots, pressing it with the back of an old spoon to avoid touching the glue. Continue gluing on clumps of moss, fitting them together like a jigsaw puzzle, until the surface is completely covered. You may prefer to wrap a large sheet of moss around the pot, securing it at the edges with glue and tearing off the excess to shape the moss to the pot.

Finishing and Maintenance

If protected with a waterproof liner, your moss container should last for several years. Over time, normal exposure to light and humidity may fade the original green color to a soft brown. To keep the moss looking fresh, spray the surface of the moss with a mixture of food coloring and water. Combine 1½ cups of water, 3 drops of green food coloring, and 1 drop of yellow food coloring in a spray bottle. Lightly mist the moss with the dye and let it dry.

Cut or tear moss strips to fit and then glue them to the inside and the outside of a wooden box.

Cover the seams with rough-cut twigs to complete the cachepot.

TOOLS

Low-temperature glue gun

Old metal spoon

Scissors or pruning shears

Spray bottle (optional)

MATERIALS

Small plant in nursery pot

Slightly larger pot, basket, or wooden box or crate (for cachepot)

Green sheet moss

Plastic saucer or plastic liner (for inside of cachepot)

Green and yellow food coloring (optional)

Bark strips, twigs, or raffia (optional, for decoration)

Low-temperature glue sticks

TIPS FOR SUCCESS

• When displaying plants in a low box or crate, line the inside and the outside of the box with moss and then place individual saucers under the pots.

• To decorate candles with moss, use candles that are 3 inches in diameter or larger to prevent the moss from catching fire. Another option is to decorate glass candle holders.

Topiary Fun

Topiary—the art of pruning plants to create formal structure in the garden—reached its height in Tudor England and was rediscovered in Victorian times. Most of today's gardens and life-styles are too casual for a high-maintenance, large-scale topiary. A touch, however, is fun. The classic examples featured here are not made from live plants—which would have to be maintained—but they give the effect of miniature living trees with flowers growing below. Because they are made with tree branches or dried flowers, they allow you to bring the look of garden topiary indoors for an extended period. A versatile decorative element, a tabletop topiary can be embellished with extra flowers, fruits, or a twist of ribbon to suit the changing seasons or to highlight a holiday celebration. Topiary decorations make lovely gifts—if you can bear to part with them.

Getting Started

Like a flower arrangement, a topiary begins with the choice of a container and the construction of a framework, including a trunk. You build it up by adding one piece of greenery or one flower at a time. The process is simple but the results are impressive. Two topiary looks are featured here: a charming moss-covered topiary (made with sheet moss from a crafts store) and an elegant magnolia-leaf topiary.

You will need a heavy pot or planter fitted with a papier-mâché liner for the base. Select a concrete urn, a clay pot, a porcelain jar, or a planter that is heavy enough to balance the weight of the top of the topiary. Purchase a papier-mâché liner for the container from a crafts store or a florist's shop. The liner should fit snugly within the base and should not be visible once it is inserted. If the liner protrudes, trim the excess height with a serrated knife. Remove the liner from the container before assembling the framework.

Bring the classic look of garden topiary indoors with an easy-to-make plant sculpture.

Pour plaster into a papier-mâché liner to anchor the trunk of a moss topiary. Slip the liner into a decorative planter.

Find a straight stick or a tree branch to serve as a trunk. Trim the stick to a point at the top.

Mix plaster of Paris with water in a plastic bucket, following the manufacturer's instructions. Pour the plaster into the liner, filling it to within 4 inches of the top. Center and insert the stick into the plaster with the pointed end up. Then insert lengths of vines, dried seedpods, and other items that would give vertical emphasis. Once the plaster dries, you can place the liner into the container.

Constructing Topiaries

These elegant topiaries will not only last all season, but also you don't have to wait for them to grow. They are assembled like any other flower arrangement, by building up from the container and by adding one dried flower or piece of greenery at a time.

Moss-Covered Topiary

To make a moss-covered topiary, use a craft foam ball 9 inches in diameter. Pierce a 4-inch-deep hole in the ball with scissors or a knife. Insert the pointed end of the stick into the hole and secure the ball with low-temperature glue. Using wire florist's pins, cover the ball with green sheet moss (available from crafts stores). Randomly pin a few thick clumps of moss to the ball for additional texture. Add berries, cockscomb, dried hydrangea, and yarrow to complete the basic topiary, securing them with florist's pins.

Dress up a topiary made from dried materials by adding fresh apples attached with wooden florist's picks and clusters of grapes anchored with wire florist's pins.

Cover the plaster at the base of the container with moss. Decorate the top of the topiary with additional materials, if desired.

For special occasions, add fresh fruits, such as grapes and apples, to the topiary for a luxurious but temporary flourish. Attach clusters of grapes with florist's pins. To secure the apples, use wooden florist's picks, inserting one end of the pick into the apple and the opposite end into the foam ball.

TOOLS

Low-temperature glue gun

Scissors or craft knife

Serrated knife

MATERIALS

9"-wide or larger container

Papier-mâché liner

24"-long stick

Vines, seedpods, or other vertical elements

Plaster of Paris

Plastic bucket

Green sheet moss

U-shaped wire florist's pins

Low-temperature glue sticks

Moss-Covered Topiary

9"-diameter craft foam ball

Dried plant materials, moss, fresh grapes and apples (optional), wooden florist's picks

Dried Magnolia Topiary

4"-diameter craft foam ball

Sheet moss, dried leaves, flowers, or potpourri

Preserved magnolia leaves

Ribbon or bow

Preserved magnolia leaves completely cover a craft foam ball to create a permanent topiary.

Dried Magnolia Topiary

To make a dried magnolia-leaf topiary, you'll need a craft foam ball 4 inches in diameter. Cut a 2-inch-deep hole in the ball with scissors or a craft knife. Place the topiary trunk into the hole and secure the ball with low-temperature glue (see **Illustration A**).

Air-dried magnolia leaves are brittle and fade to a pale gray-green or brown over time. The topiary pictured at left was made with preserved magnolia leaves, which you can order from a crafts store or a florist's shop.

To preserve your own, soak leaves in a glycerin solution. First, pound the cut ends of the magnolia branches to loosen the fibers and to promote absorption. Use a homemade solution of two parts glycerin (available at drugstores) to one part water for rich brown leaves. For dark green leaves, try a commercial preservative containing dye (available from a crafts store or a florist's shop). In either case, immerse the ends of the stems in 1 to 2 inches of solution for one to three weeks until the leaves change color and are ready to use.

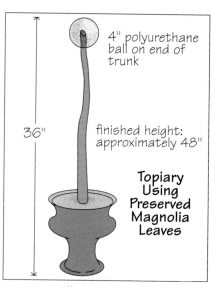

4" polyurethane ball on end of trunk

36"

finished height: approximately 48"

Topiary Using Preserved Magnolia Leaves

Illustration A

Insert the stems of the preserved leaves into the ball so that they radiate out evenly from the center and completely cover the ball. Conceal the plaster at the base of the tree with sheet moss, dried leaves, flowers, or potpourri. Pin a ribbon or a bow under the magnolia-covered ball and twist the streamers around the trunk.

Finishing and Maintenance

A topiary made from dried materials will retain a fresh look much longer if it is protected from direct sunlight and humidity. Replace dried flowers as they fade. Freshen preserved magnolia leaves by wiping with a damp cloth.

USING FRESH LEAVES AND FLOWERS

To make a short-lived topiary with fresh magnolia cuttings and flowers, choose a tree branch with three offshoots, each approximately 4 inches long (see **Illustration B**). Insert the opposite end of the branch into wet plaster. Let it dry. Moisten a block of florist's foam in water, following the manufacturer's directions. Trim the corners. Cover the foam with plastic wrap to slow down evaporation and fasten the block onto the prongs of the stick. Insert fresh magnolia cuttings into the foam.

Place the papier-mâché liner inside the decorative container. Wedge several blocks of soaked florist's foam on top of the plaster. Insert leaves and flowers into the foam at the base to cover it completely.

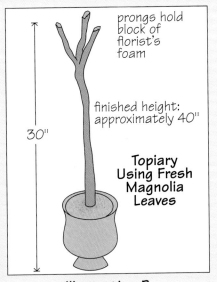

prongs hold block of florist's foam

finished height: approximately 40"

30"

Topiary Using Fresh Magnolia Leaves

Illustration B

A topiary can be an elegant centerpiece. This one is made from fresh magnolia leaves and is balanced by a base embellished with fresh flowers and greenery.

TIPS FOR SUCCESS

• To keep the topiary trunk properly positioned while the plaster dries, place the liner beside a straight chair. Tape the trunk to the edge of the chair to secure it.

• If using fresh materials for your topiary, condition cut magnolia leaves and garden flowers by letting them stand in slightly warm water for several hours.

Ivy Sculptures

TOOLS

Pliers

Wire cutters

MATERIALS

8" pot of ivy with long runners

Clay pot or decorative container

Spray paint

Florist's wire

Roll of aluminum clothesline
   wire

*Ivy twined around wire shapes transforms three potted plants
into miniature living topiaries for the tabletop.*

In the garden, versatile English ivy can be trained to climb trellises,
arbors, and obelisks to create living works of art. You can turn a
potted ivy plant into a miniature sculpture for indoor use with just a
pair of pliers, an inexpensive roll of clothesline wire, and half an
hour's time. Since the flexible aluminum wire comes already coiled,
it's easily formed into a circle or a globe. Once you understand how
the frameworks are made, it is simple to create other shapes that
resemble living topiaries.

    Spray-paint the completed wire form black, white, green, or
any desired color. Insert the form into a pot and then twist the ivy
around the wire to bring the form to life. Other plants will also work
well in this type of living sculpture: Blooming climbers, such as

jasmine or black-eyed Susan vine, and long-limbed herbs, such as rosemary, can be coaxed to follow the contours of simple wire shapes. (Fast-growing vines require regular pruning to maintain a neat, tidy form.)

Getting Started

For best results, select an ivy plant with long, unblemished runners or tendrils. Transplant the ivy into a clay pot or a decorative container. (If you can't find a pot of ivy with long runners, clip long runners from a plant growing outside. They will quickly root in a glass of water, and you can then plant them in the pot.)

1. For a wreath-shaped topiary, cut a 28-inch-long piece of clothesline wire. In the center of the wire, form a circle 12 inches in diameter. Twist the wire together at the base of the circle to secure (see **photograph 1** at right). Using the pliers, bend the free ends of the wire into a U shape 8 inches from each end. Slip one U through the other. Pinch the parallel wires together near the curve of each U so that the two ends won't slip apart. Bend the wire 4½ inches from each end to make legs for the framework.

2. To create the globe-shaped framework, make two circles, each 12 inches in diameter. Slip one circle inside the other (see **photograph 2**). Twist florist's wire around the circles at the top and the bottom to connect them. Spray-paint the framework if desired.

Finishing and Maintenance

Lift the ivy runners out of the way and insert the legs of the topiary form into the potting soil.

3. Twist the lengths of ivy around the framework, using short lengths of florist's wire to secure them to the form. Let a few runners spill over the rim of the container for a natural effect (see **photograph 3**).

1. Four twists of the pliers make a circular form with feet out of aluminum wire.

2. Two circular forms are joined by florist's wire at the top and the bottom for a globe-shaped framework.

3. Once the form is inserted into a pot and covered with ivy, small imperfections in the shape will disappear.

Dried Hydrangeas

A wide variety of colors, distinctive forms, and delicate petals give hydrangea blooms a romantic beauty all their own. These freshly cut flowers will dry to interesting shades.

TOOLS

Garden shears

Low-temperature glue gun

Wire cutters or scissors

MATERIALS

Dried hydrangea blossoms

Other dried foliage and flowers to coordinate with decorating colors used in home

Low-temperature glue sticks

Hair spray (optional)

Wire wreath

Artificial spruce garland (optional, for garland)

Floral pin holder, flower frog, crumpled chicken wire, or floral foam (optional, for dried arrangements)

Whether it's a native selection or the heirloom French type, the hydrangea is as versatile as it is beautiful. Sumptuous summer blossoms of white, lilac, pink, or purple accented by bold foliage and sculptured branches make it a prize shrub in the garden landscape. It's easy to grow as well. And then there's the decorative bonus: When dried, the flowers can be enjoyed long after summer days have passed, for they will last for several years.

In late July the flowers dry by themselves on the bush, changing to tones of antique beige and wheat brown. However, by bringing hydrangeas inside to dry before they turn, you can capture subtle hints of aqua, rose, green, and mauve and gain colorful material for winter decorations. A simple wreath of antique white hydrangeas can add a touch of garden freshness to a door or a wall.

- Always dry more hydrangeas than you think you'll need, to allow room for error.

- When selecting French hydrangeas for planting, choose shades of pink, blue, lavender, or white to coordinate with your decorating palette.

- Gently mist faded hydrangeas with pastel tints of floral spray paint to restore lifelike color.

Getting Started

The secret to drying hydrangeas lies in knowing exactly when to pick them. Summer storms and munching insects eventually take their toll on blossoms left to dry on the bush, yet the just-opened flowers will crinkle like tissue paper if they have been cut and hung to dry. Experienced gardeners watch for subtle changes of texture and color that signal the best time to pick. Over the course of the summer, the texture of the blossoms will change from soft and succulent to meaty, leathery, and finally dry and papery. Somewhere between the leather and paper stages, blossoms will lose their original intense color, taking on subtle tints of green or brownish rose. This is the ideal time to pick hydrangeas for drying.

Cut the blossoms on a warm, dry afternoon, when the moisture content of the plant will be at its lowest. Strip the leaves from the stems. The simplest way to dry the blossoms is to tie them together in loose bunches and hang them upside down in a warm, airy place out of direct sunlight. In approximately one week, when the petals rustle like paper, the blossoms are ready to be used for decoration.

Or you may prefer to stand freshly cut hydrangeas upright in a vase, with the stems immersed in 2 to 3 inches of water. The blossoms will dry as the water evaporates. Sometimes, if the humidity is low, air-drying works best; other times, drying in water in an air-conditioned room produces the best results. You may want to dry some flowers each way to be sure of an ample supply.

Working with Dried Hydrangeas

Once dry, the hydrangea blossoms can be used alone or in combination with foliage, grasses, everlastings, and other dried materials to create a variety of floral designs. The tiny stems that join the papery blossoms can be quite fragile when dry, so handle the flowers with care. You can apply hair spray to keep the blooms from shattering.

Wreaths

By attaching the dried hydrangea flowers to a wire wreath or garland base, you can make an elegant decoration that would be expensive to buy—if you could even find it. Incorporate dried leaves of various plants and include a bit of evergreen foliage for contrast. Hot glue works best for attaching the flower heads to the base.

This lovely wreath is easy to make. Just insert fresh fig leaves into the wreath and let them dry. Then add dried French hydrangea blossoms. Secure dried maypops to the wreath, using a low-temperature glue gun.

Many easy-to-grow plants make attractive companions for dried hydrangeas. This arrangement features Mexican sage, pennyroyal, and Johnson-grass as well as French hydrangeas.

Floral Arrangements

A floral arrangement is another appealing option for dried flowers. Insert the hydrangeas into a floral pin holder, a flower frog, or a handful of crumpled chicken wire placed in the bottom of a container. Or stick the stems into a block of florist's foam made for dried flower arranging. Use your imagination to create a unique display. Keep in mind that tall, slender elements, such as grasses or lavender blooms, contrast nicely with round or oval-shaped hydrangeas.

A festive garland provides a year-round accent for a collection of angels.

Garlands

To make a festive garland like the one pictured above, purchase a length of evergreen garland and trim it to the desired length. Mark the center of the swag. Starting in the middle and working to each end, attach clusters of hydrangea to the garland, using low-temperature glue. Arrange the clusters so that the resulting color pattern is symmetrical. To complete the design, make small individual bouquets of dried flowers, using cockscomb, globe amaranth, strawflower, yarrow, or whatever coordinates with your decorating scheme. Glue the bouquets to the center of the garland and at regularly spaced intervals. After the garland is hung, attach additional accents as desired.

Maintenance

High humidity and direct sunlight will rob hydrangeas and other dried flowers of their natural color. To preserve the hue and the texture as long as possible, display decorations away from direct sunlight. Refresh arrangements periodically by replacing faded flowers.

While drying hydrangeas, use the same space to dry other materials for arrangements.

17

Living Wreath

This succulent wreath thrives in a sunny location.

TOOLS

Scissors
Screwdriver

MATERIALS

Wire wreath form that separates
  into two halves

Liquid plant fertilizer

Sphagnum moss

Roll of fishing line

Several 4" containers of
  hen-and-chicks

Waterproof plate

Wreaths have adorned homes as symbols of welcome for centuries. You can easily create a living wreath that will last for a season or more by using sphagnum moss as "soil" and by selecting plants that tolerate periods of drought. Unless you are planning to water your wreath twice a day, it makes sense to use plants that have evolved to meet the challenges of an arid environment.

Succulents, such as the hen-and-chicks pictured above, send their roots into the earth in search of moisture and store excess water in thick, fleshy leaves for times of drought. They are well adapted to life on a wire wreath base packed with sphagnum moss, which can easily hold many times its weight in water. The low humidity of a typical home is also to succulents' liking. Because this type of wreath is heavy when wet, it should be displayed flat on a table. Put a plate beneath the wreath to catch excess moisture and to protect surface finishes.

Getting Started

You can make a living wreath in a morning, and it will last all season. Determine the size wreath you want and then visit a garden shop specializing in foliage plants. If you take the wreath form with you, the shopkeeper can help you decide the number of plants to purchase. Or you may prefer to use succulents that you have on hand.

Adding the Plants

This tabletop decoration is planted with hen-and-chicks, a succulent that forms small flowerlike bunches of fat, pointed leaves. Although the plants never grow to be very large, they will eventually spread and multiply to cover the entire wreath. The **photographs** at right show you how to fill the wire form with moss and insert the hen-and-chicks.

Place the completed wreath on a waterproof plate to protect the tabletop from excess moisture.

Finishing and Maintenance

A succulent wreath needs a warm room where it will receive full sunlight. Wait until the moss has dried out completely before watering. Water less often in the winter than in the summer.

TIPS FOR SUCCESS
❖

- To make the wreath grow symmetrically, give it a quarter turn from time to time so that all the plants will have equal exposure to the light.

- Move the wreath to the dinner table for use as a temporary centerpiece, inserting water picks with flowers for added color.

MAKING A LIVE WREATH

1. Mix liquid fertilizer with water, according to label directions. Soak moss in the solution and squeeze out excess moisture. Separate the form into halves. Fill one-half with sphagnum moss.

2. Place the second half of the form over the moss-filled half. Secure with fishing line.

3. Remove the succulents from their containers, retaining as much of their root system as possible. Pierce the moss with a screwdriver and insert the roots of a plant.

4. Continue piercing and then adding plants until all are in place. Tuck in additional pieces of moss to cover the wire frame.

Painted Pots

A luxuriant crop of new grass looks great in this painted and sand-speckled pot.

TOOLS

Paintbrushes or disposable sponge brushes

Sandpaper

Tray or box to hold sand (optional)

MATERIALS

Clay pots

Exterior latex paints

Sand

Clear acrylic spray

Orange shellac or polyurethane

Denatured alcohol (for shellac cleanup)

An inexpensive terra-cotta pot is functional but undistinguished. However, a coat of paint and a sprinkling of sand can quickly add personality and flair. You don't have to be an artist to make a pot look like a work of art. And because you are not limited to the colors another designer picked out, you can put together any combination you desire. This enables you to customize a group of potted plants to complement the decor of a sun-room, a porch, a kitchen, a bathroom—anywhere that can use a splash of color. Pots can also serve as containers for gifts.

Getting Started

For each pot, you'll need two contrasting colors of exterior latex paint.

1. Paint the interior and the lip of the pot with one color and let it dry. Sand the lip of the pot lightly to let some of the terra-cotta show through and to create the illusion of a gently aged treasure. Paint the sides and the bottom of the pot with a contrasting shade (see **photograph 1** at right).

2. While the paint is still wet on the sides, roll the pot in dry sand or sprinkle sand evenly over the paint (see **photograph 2**). Let the paint dry. Then apply a coat of clear acrylic spray to the interior and the exterior of the pot to seal the finish and to help the sand adhere.

3. When the acrylic spray has dried, apply a coat of orange shellac or polyurethane to all surfaces of the pot (see **photograph 3**). Let this dry completely before using the pot. The resulting finish should remain in good condition for several years.

Displaying the Pots

Although these make great planters, the pots are decorative all by themselves. Display the pots individually, grouped on a tray, or lined up along a mantel or in a window.

TIPS FOR SUCCESS

- To keep costs down, use latex paint left over from painting the exterior of your house.

- Vary the texture of the sand used from fine to coarse to produce effects from elegant to rustic.

PAINTING A POT

1. When the interior and the lip of the pot have dried, paint the exterior of the pot with a contrasting shade.

2. Roll the wet pot in sand or sprinkle sand over the exterior to soften the color and to texturize the paint.

3. Apply a coat of orange shellac or polyurethane to all surfaces of the pot for protection.

Picket-Fence Plant Stand

This plant stand organizes several potted plants at window level, allowing them to brighten a room while spending the winter indoors.

TIPS FOR SUCCESS

❖

- Not all prefabricated fencing sections are equally well made, so carefully inspect the sections for splitting, splintering, warping, and overall quality before purchasing.

- Predrill holes for screws to avoid splitting the wood.

- In the summer, take the plant stand outside and fill it with flowers. Use it on the patio, under a window, or as a window box.

When you bring your potted herbs, tender perennials, and container plants inside during the fall, there never seems to be enough room for them to sit where they can get the sunlight they need to remain healthy. Most windowsills aren't deep enough to hold large pots. Purchased plant stands can be quite expensive, and many aren't designed to hold more than one pot. You can solve this problem beautifully—and inexpensively—by making a plant stand from prefabricated picket fencing.

To save time sawing and nailing, buy a section of fencing ready-made and modify it to hold a plant shelf. The design pictured above requires only basic woodworking skills and tools. Our planter was made from an 8-foot-long section of fencing and frames a 42-inch-wide window. If your window and the fencing you select have different measurements, adapt the following instructions to suit.

Getting Started

Several picket styles are available; select the one that works best with the trim and the furnishings of your room.

1. Hold the section of fencing against your window and determine how high you'd like the plant stand to be. Remember that the tops of the pots must be level with or above the windowsill in order to receive the maximum amount of sunlight. You can safely cut off all or part of the picket length below the bottom stringer, but leave the stringer intact to keep the plant stand stable. Mark the cutting line and use a handsaw to cut off the excess length.

2. Decide how wide you want the plant stand to be. Cut the front section of the plant stand at least a couple of inches wider than the overall width of the window plus its trim in order to "frame" the window. Plan your cuts to avoid sawing through a picket. Make sure the two sides of the panel are symmetrical; you may have to adjust the panel size slightly to achieve this. Mark the cutting lines and trim the sides.

3. From the leftover fencing, cut two side panels, each at least 11½ inches wide. Next, cut two small pieces from the wood removed from the bottom of the fence to make supports for the shelf. Attach one to the inside of each side panel 16 inches from the top of the pickets (see the **illustration**). Attach the side panels to the front panel with metal corner braces screwed to the stringers.

4. Measure the distance between the side panels on the inside of the plant stand. Cut the two 2 x 4s to this length to rest on the supports. Attach the boards to the supports to make the slatted plant shelf.

Finishing and Maintenance

Sand the plant stand to smooth the wood, if desired. Paint or stain and varnish the wood to protect it from water damage.

TOOLS

Drill with appropriate bits

Hammer

Handsaw

Paintbrushes

Screwdriver

Tape measure

MATERIALS

One 42" x 96" section of prefabricated picket fencing

Two 2 x 4s long enough for wooden slats

4 metal inside corner braces

8 wood screws (for braces)

6-penny nails

Sandpaper (optional)

Exterior latex paint or stain and varnish

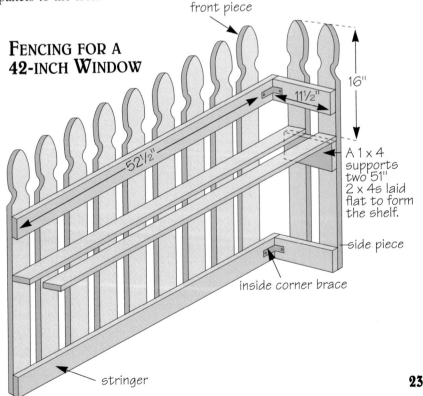

FENCING FOR A 42-INCH WINDOW

front piece

16"

11½"

52½"

A 1 x 4 supports two 51" 2 x 4s laid flat to form the shelf.

side piece

inside corner brace

stringer

Accent with Lights

An uplight placed in a clay pot adds decorative lighting to a grouping of houseplants.

TOOLS

Sharp scissors or wire cutters
Small screwdriver

MATERIALS

Decorative Uplight

Uplight

Clay pot or concrete planter (larger than uplight) with drainage hole

Replacement electrical plug (with instructions)

4 adhesive-backed rubber pads (¼" or thicker)

Low-voltage transformer

An uplight placed among potted plants can bring drama to an area by beaming upward to emphasize the geometry of the foliage. Coming from an unexpected angle, this light casts intriguing shadows on walls, ceilings, and fences. The trick is finding a light that appears to belong in a garden setting; many of those available are stark, modern fixtures. This problem is easily solved by putting the uplight inside a clay pot or a decorative concrete planter that would be right at home in a garden.

Getting Started

The floor-standing uplight shown at left was placed in a clay pot that blends with the display of baskets and plants. If you like, you can simply set the light in the pot and drape the cord over the edge. For a more finished look, take just a few minutes to modify the light's wiring and to run the cord out through the drainage hole at the bottom of the pot.

The same principle can be adapted to create an outside light. But instead of a light powered by household current, this version uses a low-voltage transformer for outdoor landscape lighting.

Although you don't have to use low voltage, it is much safer for do-it-yourselfers to install. Also, it's relatively inexpensive, and you can find a wide range of fixtures.

Decorative Uplight

Select a pot or a planter that is slightly taller and wider than the uplight so that the light will nest inside it, out of sight. At a hardware store, purchase a replacement electrical plug that is packaged with instructions. You'll also need four ¼-inch-thick or thicker adhesive-backed rubber pads to elevate the bottom of the pot.

Attach the rubber pads at regular intervals around the bottom of the pot. With the light unplugged, cut the plug from the cord, using sharp scissors or wire cutters. If the cord has a line switch, remove that as well. Loosen the screw with a small screwdriver and then separate the two halves of the switch. Make note of how the electrical cord is arranged inside the switch, with one of the wires cut in half and the halves separated by the structure of the switch. You will need to arrange the cord in this way when you replace the switch.

Next, run the cord through the drainage hole in the bottom of the pot and replace the line switch. Following the manufacturer's instructions, attach the replacement plug to the end of the electrical cord. Position your new uplight beside any plant you'd like to emphasize with dramatic lighting.

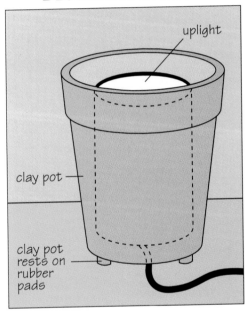

DECORATIVE UPLIGHT

uplight

clay pot

clay pot rests on rubber pads

TOOLS

Drill with appropriate bits (optional)

Handsaw

Sharp scissors or wire cutters

Small screwdriver

Low-voltage light fixtures can be modified easily to make an uplight that can be used outdoors.

MATERIALS

Outdoor Uplight

7-watt mini floodlight

Low-voltage transformer

Clay pot or concrete planter (larger than uplight) with drainage hole

Replacement electrical plug (with instructions)

Small amount of gravel

Nail and hook or fastener (optional)

Outdoor Uplight

The light pictured below was made from a 12-inch terra-cotta wall planter. Select a pot or a decorative container that will resist the effects of moisture and winter weather. You'll also need a low-voltage light fixture for outdoor landscape lighting, a low-voltage transformer, a handsaw, and some gravel. If you intend to hang the fixture, you'll need a nail and a hook or a fastener large enough to handle the weight of the container, plus gravel.

A 7-watt mini floodlight will work well as the uplight for this project. If it has an anchor spike at the base, saw it off. Place the floodlight in the pot and run the cord through the drainage hole at the bottom of the pot. Put some gravel into the pot to stabilize the light. Connect the wiring to the transformer to be sure it is working properly. Follow the manufacturer's instructions to make the necessary connections.

To install a hanging light, first disconnect the light from the transformer. Decide where you want to hang the light and mark the position. Attach the hanger and then hang the light. If the fixture is hung on a fence, hide the cord by drilling a hole and pulling it to the other side. On a solid wall, let the cord dangle and conceal it behind a plant.

Once you have the light positioned, install the transformer according to the manufacturer's instructions.

Lush foliage conceals the wiring of an uplight placed in a terra-cotta wall planter.

Strictly Horticultural

Every garden offers a multitude of opportunities for weekend projects. Often these are related to crafts or construction, but some may be horticultural, having long-lasting, positive effects on a garden. Whether undertaken out of necessity or just out of a desire to make a cherished haven look better, these efforts are more fruitful if done properly. In tackling some of the projects in this section, you will sharpen your gardening skills while enhancing the beauty of your garden.

Planting a Memory Tree not only describes how to properly plant a tree but also suggests a way of getting family members involved in gardening. When you plant a tree to mark a birth, a wedding, or even a death, you create a wonderful living tribute to a loved one.

Establishing a Ground Cover suggests what to do with areas in which grass will not grow. You can solve a nagging problem and at the same time provide the garden with color, texture, and low-maintenance foliage. Once you have grown ground covers, you'll discover even more ways to use them effectively in the garden.

Repairing Your Lawn with Sod tells you how to do easy patch jobs on unsightly dead spots that inevitably appear in otherwise carefully manicured lawns. Think of this knowledge as insurance that helps you protect a valuable landscaping investment.

Pruning Shrubs into Trees provides information on how you can convert an overgrown shrub into an attractive small tree by using the proper pruning techniques. **Pruning Crepe Myrtle** follows up on this theme. The approaches described can be applied to other shrubs and trees as well to give your garden a healthy, well-kept overall appearance.

Finally, **Transplanting Trees and Shrubs** details how to move plants from one spot to another successfully. Suggestions for preliminary root pruning, as well as digging the plant and transporting the heavy root ball, make a difficult job much easier. These hints also increase the plant's chances of survival, which is important in the case of a beloved or valuable tree.

This newly planted Green Mountain sugar maple will sport bright yellow foliage in the fall.

Planting a Memory Tree

A tree planted in honor of a person or an event becomes a living monument.

TOOLS

Garden fork

Hose

Knife (optional)

Pick or mattock

Round-point shovel

Tarp, large flattened cardboard box, or other suitable material on which to put the soil that is removed from the hole

MATERIALS

Proper tree for the planting site

Controlled-release fertilizer

Compost or leaf mold (optional, for sandy soils)

Sand and organic matter, such as compost or leaf mold (optional, for clay soils)

Trees set the stage for a garden. Over time, they build its character. In the summer they provide cooling shade; in the winter their bark and branches add visual interest, and wildlife may benefit from their greenery or berries. Trees with showy flowers or fall leaf color hold seasonal displays that are worth waiting for all year.

Yet trees can be more than integral parts of the landscape. They can be important parts of our lives when they are planted as living monuments to people or to events. Some families have a tradition of planting a tree to celebrate a birth, while others plant a tree to mark the end of a life. Still others plant trees for wedding anniversaries or for special birthdays. Try to include various family members in the tree-planting project and document the activity. Then watch young family members and the trees grow up together.

Because many trees live for generations, it is important to do the planting job right to avoid problems later on.

Getting Started

Long-lived trees, such as American holly, Canadian hemlock, ginkgo, Southern magnolia, and white oak, are often planted as memory trees. If you have a small yard or garden, however, consider a more compact tree that will live for many years, such as a Japanese maple, redbud, saucer magnolia, Savannah holly, or serviceberry.

It's critical to match the right tree with the right spot. A memory tree is usually a specimen tree, so choose a suitably prominent place to plant it. Look out for power lines, roof overhangs, or nearby established trees and shrubs. Then consider the ground where the tree will be planted. Tree roots will extend far beyond the hole in which a small tree is first planted. Water lines, sewer pipes, and other buried utilities can also pose problems. If you're not sure where these are located, call the utility company or the water department and ask about having lines marked for you.

Late fall and early winter are the best times to plant trees. Roots develop even in the winter, when the plant has a chance to establish itself before the heavy demands of the growing season. You can also successfully plant a tree in the spring if you water during dry periods. The chance of a favorable outcome with summer plantings is much smaller.

Planting

Most of the trees available at retail centers are container grown or balled and burlapped. Some trees, especially those bought from catalogs or forestry nurseries, may be available as bare-root seedlings. Planting techniques are basically the same for all three forms. Of course, there is no root ball with bare-root seedlings. In their case, it is extremely important not to expose the roots to drying wind and to sunlight during the planting process. Instead, leave them covered with moist material until the hole is prepared; then plant and cover the roots with soil as quickly as possible.

TIPS FOR SUCCESS

• As you remove soil from the hole, place it on a tarp, on a large flattened cardboard box, or in a wheelbarrow to make cleanup easier. A tarp or a wheelbarrow can be helpful for mixing sand, organic material, or fertilizer as well.

• Be sure to water your new tree during dry spells throughout the first year. Watch closely for signs of drought in the spring and the summer. After a year, the tree should be well established and be able to withstand all but the most severe dry periods.

PLANTING A SMALL TREE

1. Dig a hole at least three times as wide as the root ball—the wider the better.

2. Lay a shovel handle across the hole to help you set the top of the root ball flush or slightly higher than the surrounding soil.

3. Add fertilizer, organic material, and sand to the backfill as needed.

1. Dig a hole at least three times as wide as the root ball but no deeper than the root ball is high (see **photograph 1** at left). There is no exact formula; three times is generally a minimum, five times is best.

2. When the tree is set in the hole, the top of the root ball should be level with or slightly higher than the ground (see **photograph 2**). If the top of the root ball is too low, remove the tree and shovel some soil back into the hole.

3. If your soil is excessively sandy, mix equal parts of compost or leaf mold with native soil to fill the hole around the root ball. This will enhance water retention, keeping your tree from drying out too quickly. If the soil is heavy clay, improve the drainage by mixing one-third sand and one-third organic matter with native soil. In either case, it helps to add a cupful of controlled-release tree fertilizer, such as 12-6-6, to the soil mix (see **photograph 3**).

4. For a container-grown tree, remove it from the plastic container or wire basket. If the tree is root bound, you will need to use a shovel or a knife to loosen the root ball, making a vertical cut in the bottom and slicing approximately a third of the way up (see **photograph 4** at right). Pull the halves apart approximately an inch before setting the root ball in the hole.

If the tree is balled and burlapped, leave the burlap wrapped around the root ball but be sure to take off all synthetic ties and metal fasteners. If a non-biodegradable fabric was used instead of burlap, carefully remove it before placing the tree in the hole.

To plant a bare-root tree, first prepare a mound of soil in the shape of a cone at the bottom of the hole. Remove the tree from the moist packing material and spread the roots out evenly over the cone. Hold the base of the tree at ground level while you fill in around the roots with soil. A cone will not work for a bare-root tree with a long tap root. In this case, dig the hole deep enough so that the tap root does not bend in the shape of a J.

As you fill the hole with soil, take care not to leave any unfilled pockets of air around the roots. Tamp the soil but do not pack it tightly.

Finishing

5. Water your new tree thoroughly and mulch the entire area with a 2- to 4-inch-deep layer of organic material, such as shredded bark or pine straw (see **photograph 5**).

4. Make a single vertical cut through the root ball, cutting about a third of the way up from the bottom.

5. After watering your tree, mulch with shredded bark or pine straw.

Top-heavy evergreens, such as this magnolia, need to be supported with stakes.

31

Establishing a Ground Cover

Mondo grass will form a thick carpet in two to three years after planting.

TOOLS

Mattock or other planting tool

Tiller or garden fork

MATERIALS

Nonselective herbicide

Appropriate ground cover plant for site

1 x 4 or 1 x 6 board, 8' to 10' long

Shredded bark mulch

Organic material

Coarse sand (optional, for hard, compacted soil)

Controlled-release fertilizer

The most rewarding projects are simple ones that resolve long-standing problems and enhance the garden at the same time. If you are tired of looking at a bare spot, a barren hillside, or a washed-out area, get creative with a ground cover. Such a planting brings interesting texture and color to the garden and generally requires little maintenance. Many also perform well in the shade, where grass will not grow. Individual evergreen ground cover sprigs planted in a mass will weave into a natural, lush carpet in only a couple of years.

Getting Started

An assortment of excellent ground covers is available for a variety of growing conditions. Some ground covers, such as mondo grass, liriope, and ajuga, will tolerate more sunlight than others. If you have a steep slope, you may want to plant common periwinkle, creeping juniper, English ivy, or Japanese star jasmine. And for delicate color, choose the shade-loving Lenten rose, which produces light pink or white blooms from February through May.

Whatever you select, remember that weeds are the number one enemy of any newly planted ground cover. Once you have chosen an area you want to plant, get a head start on weed control by spraying the area with a nonselective herbicide, such as Roundup or Finale. Plan ahead, as it takes several days for the results of each spraying to become evident.

Planting

Take time to prepare the soil so that the ground cover roots properly. Liriope, mondo grass, and pachysandra roots need loose soil to move underground and to multiply. Till the soil to a depth of 4 to 6 inches. Add plenty of organic matter, such as peat moss, leaf mold, or bark. If the soil is hard and compacted, add coarse sand as well.

If the area to be planted is too steep to till, consider planting common periwinkle, a creeping variety of juniper, English ivy, or Japanese star jasmine that will spread on top of the ground. In this case, kill the existing grass or weeds on the slope, removing only vines or woody plants that get in your way. Don't till but simply plant through the dead vegetation. This will hold the soil in place while the new ground cover is getting established. (Common periwinkle and English ivy are invasive. Plant them in areas where they cannot overtake other plants.) When planting these types of ground cover, sprinkle a little controlled-release fertilizer into each hole.

Before You Plant

1. Select containers that are full when purchasing ground covers, such as mondo grass or liriope.

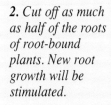

2. Cut off as much as half of the roots of root-bound plants. New root growth will be stimulated.

3. Divide plants such as mondo grass and liriope into several sprigs per cell pack. Groom the plants by removing any dead foliage.

4. Use a board marked with the appropriate spacing to keep rows straight. This will help the ground cover to close over the area evenly.

Before buying ground cover plants, check with friends and neighbors. Many ground covers multiply and spread easily, and other gardeners may have a generous supply of plants to share. (See **photographs 1–4** on page 33 for step-by-step directions on planting ground covers.)

Plant in a gridlike pattern, as this will make your planting look neat and orderly and will allow your ground cover to fill in evenly. On one edge of a board, make marks according to the recommended spacing for your selected ground cover (see the **chart** at right); stagger the marks along the opposite edge. This marked board will help you line up the sprigs.

Finishing

When finished planting, add a 2- to 3-inch-deep layer of shredded bark mulch to the beds. Mulching keeps moisture in and weeds out. For the first couple of years, before your ground cover fills in, it is critical to keep the beds free of weeds. Once weeds become established, they are almost impossible to remove. On the other hand, once the ground cover plants take over the area, they will choke out most weeds.

TIPS FOR SUCCESS

❖

- Avoid summer planting.
- Keep plants well watered until they are firmly established.

GROUND COVER SPACING

Ground cover plants set out at the specific spacings given below will fill in their areas in two to three years. The time will vary according to soil type, fertilization, and irrigation.

PLANT	RECOMMENDED SPACING
Ajuga (*Ajuga* species)	8 inches
Common periwinkle (*Vinca minor*)	12 inches
Creeping rosemary (*Rosmarinus officinalis* Prostratus)	18 inches
Dwarf juniper (*Juniperus chinensis* Procumbens Nana)	36 inches
English ivy (*Hedera helix*)	14 to 18 inches
Japanese ardisia (*Ardisia japonica*)	6 to 8 inches
Japanese pachysandra (*Pachysandra terminalis*)	8 to 10 inches
Japanese star jasmine (*Trachelospermum asiaticum*)	24 inches
Lenten rose (*Helleborus orientalis*)	14 to 16 inches
Liriope (*Liriope* species)	8 to 12 inches
Mondo grass (*Ophiopogon japonicus*)	6 inches
Wild ginger (*Asarum canadense*)	4 inches
Wintercreeper (*Euonymus radicans*)	12 inches

Repairing Your Lawn with Sod

The beginning of the growing season is the ideal time to patch your lawn.

E ven a carefully manicured lawn is likely to have an unsightly dead spot sooner or later. Just one such place can detract from its overall beauty, and if left unchecked, the area may eventually affect the health of the lawn. Fortunately, a grass patch job is quick and easy.

Getting Started

Causes of grass dying out in a particular spot in your lawn can range from pets to fungus to fire from a barbecue grill. Before the area is patched, find out what the culprit is. Your local County Extension Service office can help you diagnose the problem and plan some preventive maintenance.

Lawns can be patched almost any time during the growing season, though success may be hard to achieve in the summer due to high temperatures and dry conditions. New sod needs plenty of water all year.

TOOLS

Bow rake

Garden fork

Hose and sprinkler

Sod cutter or sharp spade

MATERIALS

Certified sod matched to lawn to cover damaged area

Controlled-release fertilizer

LAWN REPAIR WITH SOD

1. Select firm, green strips no more than 1 inch thick.

2. Using a garden fork, loosen the soil in the patch area to a depth of at least 8 inches.

3. Position the new sod so that the joints around the strips are as tight as possible.

First, purchase replacement sod. Check with local garden centers, nurseries, and sod farms for a reliable source of high-quality certified sod. *Certified* means the sod is guaranteed to be free of pests and noxious weeds. Be sure to match the type of sod to the grass type that you already have. (If you are unsure of the type you have, take a sample to a local garden center.)

When buying sod, look for firm, sturdy pieces that don't pull apart when lifted (see **photograph 1** at left). The strips should be moist and green, not dry and yellow or brown, and no more than 1 inch thick. The roots in strips with a thick layer of soil on the bottom take much longer to knit into the surrounding lawn.

Making the Patch

1. Remove the dead sod with a sod cutter or a sharp spade, making a straight and definite cut. After the old sod has been removed, loosen the exposed soil with a garden fork to a depth of at least 8 inches. Loose, well-aerated soil is key to growing healthy grass.

2. Level the soil with a bow rake, working the soil so that the surface is smooth. Place the new sod strips on top of the soil and make sure that the joints are as tight as possible around the sod strips, as well as between the sod strips and the existing lawn. Tamp the new sod lightly with your foot for good contact with the soil.

Water thoroughly right away and then every day for the next two weeks.

TIPS FOR SUCCESS
❖

• Fill the joints around the sod strips with fine sand to assist the strips in knitting together.

• Use fertilizer to help roots develop quickly.

• If you have to store the strips at home until you have time to complete the patch job, place them in a lightly shaded spot and keep them moist. Do not pile strips on top of each other.

Pruning Shrubs into Trees

You can transform an overlooked and forgotten Burford holly into an attractive treelike feature by removing its lower branches.

Many shrubs start out as small, innocent-looking plants but eventually grow into unwieldy giants. Years ago, when Burford holly was being touted as a can't-miss shrub, homeowners had no idea that one could grow 25 feet tall or more.

With proper pruning and a little relandscaping, an overgrown Burford holly and other shrubs not easily managed can be transformed into attractive small trees that give an established look to the garden without dwarfing everything around them.

Expose the target plant by removing the overgrowth that surrounds it.

TOOLS

Lopping shears or pruning shears

Pruning saw

Shovel

MATERIALS

Ground cover or slow-growing,
    shade-tolerant plants

Mulch

Getting Started

It would seem difficult to hide a 25-foot shrub, but many times such a healthy specimen is choked by other overgrown shrubs. If you have a large mass of vegetation, no single plant draws the eye, so everything goes unnoticed.

If this is the case, the first thing to do is dig up the surrounding plants and move them to a more appropriate location. Then the main shrub—soon to be a tree—will become visible. Winter is the best time to transplant and to prune your existing shrub. Trees and shrubs are dormant during this season, and deciduous species have lost most or all of their leaves. Also, with the leaves gone, it is easier to see which limbs need to be removed.

SHRUBS TO TREES

Other shrubs besides Burford holly sometimes become overgrown and are candidates for transformation into trees. They include the following:

Azalea

Chaste tree

Ligustrum

Rhododendron

Rose-of-Sharon

Viburnum

Vitex

Waxleaf privet

Wax myrtle

Winged euonymus

Wax myrtle is one of the more popular evergreen shrubs often used as a small tree.

After you have decided which limbs should go, begin pruning by removing all the limbs that are damaged or dead. Next, cut off all branches that are 2 inches in diameter and smaller, up to a height of 5 feet. With the lines of the trunk exposed, the shrub will start to look more like a tree.

Proper Pruning Techniques

Do not cut branches flush with the trunk, as this leaves the plant susceptible to fungus and pests. Instead, cut back only as far as the *branch collar,* the raised or swollen area at the base of the branch where it joins the trunk. (On many trees—less so on shrubs—this collar appears as a knob of concentric rings of bark.) The collar forms a protective barrier against disease and pests. It also promotes healing of the wound caused by pruning.

Small limbs and branches, up to about 1½ inches in diameter, can be cut with lopping shears or pruning shears. Larger limbs should be cut with a pruning saw. When using a saw, make three cuts for each branch removed (see the **illustrations** at right). Make the first cut on the underside of the branch, approximately 6 to 8 inches from the collar. Cut about a fourth of the way through. Make the second cut on the top side, 1 to 2 inches farther out than the undercut, cutting the branch through. Because of the first protective cut, the branch will fall without any bark tearing away. Finally, cut the remaining branch back to the collar. (Don't bother painting the cut unless you are pruning an oak. Research shows that tree paint does little except prevent oak wilt.)

Finishing

Shade cast by the largest, most dense shrubs may keep grass from growing underneath them. This is a great place, however, to be creative with ground covers (see **Establishing a Ground Cover** on page 32) or other low-growing, shade-tolerant perennials, such as hosta or Lenten rose. Or you can take a low-maintenance approach and encircle its base with a neat ring of mulch.

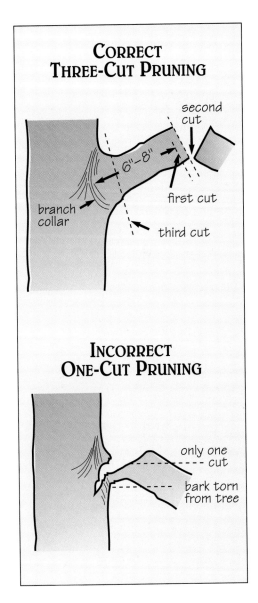

CORRECT THREE-CUT PRUNING

second cut

6"–8"

first cut

branch collar

third cut

INCORRECT ONE-CUT PRUNING

only one cut

bark torn from tree

Pruning Crepe Myrtle

Pruned crepe myrtles grow to be small multitrunked trees.

TOOLS

Lopping shears or pruning
 shears

Pruning saw

Named for its soft, crinkly blossoms, crepe myrtle is a small Asian tree that greets the summer with a colorful display. After blooms and leaves have fallen, crepe myrtle's thin, paperlike bark peels away to reveal satiny smooth trunks, making the tree an asset even in the winter—that is, unless it has been improperly pruned. Amputated, knuckled, and disfigured branches mar the tree's outline and detract from its appearance.

Since crepe myrtle is a multitrunked tree that sends up numerous shoots or suckers from its base, it requires some pruning almost every year. But if the tree is trained properly, it will need only minimal pruning as it ages.

Getting Started

It is important to realize that pruning the top of a crepe myrtle is not a solution for a tree that is too big. Pruning to reduce height can only be a maintenance struggle that you will never win. Fortunately, even large crepe myrtles can be transplanted successfully. Replace them with shorter selections that are better suited to the site.

If you prune heavily to make your crepe myrtle bloom, you are fighting another losing battle. Contrary to common belief, you cannot stimulate flowering with any pruning other than by tip-pruning the ends of branches in late summer. If your crepe myrtle is not blooming well, it may be getting too much shade. Try moving the tree into the sunlight. You can encourage trees in the lower and coastal South to produce a smaller second flush of blooms by pruning the old blossoms as they fade, but heavy pruning in the winter has no bearing on this.

However, pruning a scraggly tree can produce good results. Multiple trunks are handsome, but too many can make the tree appear unkempt. If you prune to shape the tree, remember this rule of thumb: Don't cut to see over it; cut to see through it.

Pruning Techniques

With the proper techniques, you can correct old pruning problems and avoid future pitfalls. Cut limbs back to the **branch collar,** the raised or swollen area at the base of the branch where it joins the trunk. This collar appears as a knob of concentric rings of bark. It forms a protective barrier against disease and insects and promotes healing of the wound that results from pruning.

Limbs that are too large for lopping shears or pruning shears require three cuts with a pruning saw. Make the first cut on the underside of the branch, approximately 6 to 8 inches from the collar. Cut about a fourth of the way through. Then make the second cut on the top side, 1 to 2 inches farther out than the

The smooth bark of a crepe myrtle is displayed when the tree is properly pruned.

41

REMOVING LIMBS

1. Large limbs require three cuts with a pruning saw. First make an undercut 6 to 8 inches from the collar.

2. Next, make another cut 1 to 2 inches farther out the limb, sawing through the limb.

3. Finally, saw off the remaining stub just outside the branch collar.

undercut, cutting the branch through. Because of the first protective cut, the branch will fall without any bark being torn away. Finally, cut the remaining branch back to the collar (see **photographs 1–3** at left or the **illustration** on page 39). Don't bother painting the cut, as little is gained by doing so.

Pruning

Middle to late winter is the best time to prune a crepe myrtle because the leaves have dropped and the tree is dormant. Also, it is easier to see which branches need to be removed.

Start at the base of the plant. If the tree is young and is getting its first pruning, select three to five of the straighter, thicker stems to become the tree's main trunks. The stems should be evenly spaced and fan outward in a vase shape. Old trees may have several basal sprouts or suckers that should be removed. Young trees can be trained to a single trunk if you prefer a more formal look.

When the base has been pruned, move up the tree and remove all spindly growth from the main stalks, up to a height of at least 5 to 6 feet. This helps show off the smooth bark, establishes a strong form, and allows air to circulate freely through the branches, reducing the chances of mildew. If the tree is less than 5 feet tall, remove spindly growth from the bottom to the top.

After this growth has been removed, prune all the branches on the main trunks, up to 3 feet. Above 3 feet, remove limbs so that the remaining branches are spaced no closer than 6 to 8 inches apart.

If past prunings have left stubs from

Remove all spindly growth from the main trunks, up to a height of 5 to 6 feet.

which two shoots sprouted, use pruning shears to correct the problem. For each stub, remove one of the shoots. Then cut the stub back to the remaining stem. The two almost-flush cuts should heal over together (see **photographs 1–4** at right).

Although some gardeners prefer to remove brown seedpods that formed after the plant flowered the previous summer, this is not mandatory, as leaving them on will not reduce flowering the next year. However, short branches that are curved downward from the weight of the flowers should be shortened. Prune each to an outward-facing bud so that the new branch will grow up and out of—not into—the center.

Sometimes a tree has been pruned so badly in the past that you may have to cut it back to the ground. As drastic as this sounds, the tree will develop in only two or three years because the established root system will support rapid growth. When the new shoots appear, select the ones that are strong and well placed and remove all the others. You may have to remove suckers several times during the growing season and support the long, limber shoots with stakes during the first year.

CREPE MYRTLES COME IN ALL SIZES

If you need to replace a crepe myrtle, get a new one that best suits the area in which it will be planted. Semidwarf selections reach 8 to 14 feet in about 10 years. Varieties include Acoma, Catawba, Cherokee, Comanche, Hopi, and Sioux. Biloxi, Byers Wonderful White, Dallas Red, Fantasy, Natchez, Muskogee, and Watermelon Red all grow to at least 20 feet, so plant them where their height will be an asset. Consider Centennial, Hope, Prairie Lace, or Victor if you want a shrub that will grow only 3 to 4 feet tall.

PRUNING PROPERLY

1. A common pruning error is to leave a long stub, which produces double shoots.

2. To correct this problem, first remove one of the shoots.

3. Then cut out the stub.

4. The resulting wound will heal over, and one stem will be left.

Transplanting Trees and Shrubs

Moving a tree as large as this crepe myrtle is a two-person job.

No matter how well you plan your garden, there will always come a time when you will need to transplant something. Maybe a tree or a shrub has grown larger than you expected, and a more spacious location is needed. Perhaps an addition to the house or a new deck has made it necessary to relocate a favorite flowering tree. Or a tree may have been cut or struck down, causing too much sunlight to fall on a shade-loving shrub; conversely, a crepe myrtle may be getting left in the shade by neighboring trees.

While a bit labor intensive, digging up and moving perennials and small shrubs is a relatively simple and straightforward process. Relocating a large shrub or a small tree, on the other hand, can be both a major task for you and a rather risky operation for the plant. However, by following a few basic principles, you can reduce the work load and, at the same time, greatly increase the chances of the plant's survival.

TOOLS

Marking paint

Mattock

Sharp spade or shovel

Stakes

MATERIALS

Hose

Tarp (optional, for large shrubs and small trees)

Wheelbarrow or garden cart (optional, for large plants)

Getting Started

When you have decided that a particular shrub or small tree needs to be moved, the first step is to select a new location. Consider the sunlight and shade requirements of the transplant, along with the impact that surrounding trees and other plants will have on the new arrival and vice versa.

Next, determine the diameter of the root ball of the plant to be moved. In general, a plant has a root ball about equal to its spread. However, it is impossible to dig such a large root ball with shrubs and small trees. The size of a tree's root ball is determined by the diameter of the tree's trunk. Ideally, you should allow 9 to 12 inches of diameter on the root ball for every 1 inch of the trunk's diameter. (Measure the trunk's diameter at about 4 feet above the ground. For trees with multiple trunks, combine the diameters of all the trunks.)

TIPS FOR SUCCESS

• In sizing up the job ahead, remember that soil can weigh more than 100 pounds per cubic foot. Don't dig up more than you can carry. Hire a professional for large jobs, or at least be sure to have plenty of help on hand.

• Large shrubs and trees tend to suffer more significant transplant shock than smaller plants. This is because a good portion of the large shrub or tree's root system is likely to be left behind. Pruning can reduce the shock to the tree by helping to restore the proper ratio of branches to roots. When you prune, be sure to maintain the shape of the plant and to remove any branches that were injured in the move.

Many small shrubs can be transplanted without root pruning.

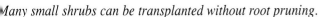

When transplanting a small shrub, dig a root ball about equal to the spread of the plant.

45

ADVANCE ROOT PRUNING

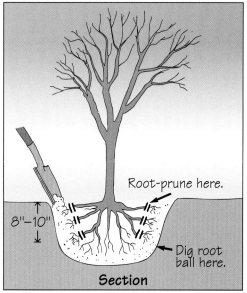

Advance root pruning can greatly increase the chances of the plant's survival by promoting development of new feeder roots that will be moved with the root ball.

Planning and timing are very important for successful transplanting. The best time to make the actual move is in the winter, when the plant is dormant. This is crucial for roses, which do not survive moving very well if they are transplanted when in full leaf (see the **box** on page 48). Ideally, you should prepare the plant for the move by root-pruning months in advance. This is especially true of trees and large shrubs. Small shrubs generally do not need to be root-pruned.

Root pruning severs lateral roots so that new, fine roots will sprout. The pruning is done within the soil that will be part of the root ball when the plant is dug up so that the new roots will be taken with the tree.

Prune the roots in the fall before the move. Use marking paint to draw a circular outline of the root ball on the ground around the plant. This is the root-ball line. Then draw a second broken-line circle 3 to 4 inches inside the first circle. This is the root-pruning line. To make the cuts to the roots, using a sharp spade or shovel, cut 8 to 10 inches deep along the root-pruning line on just half of the circle. Water daily for three to four weeks. Then cut around the other half of the circle and water daily for another three to four weeks (see the **illustration** at left). The tree may require staking if it seems unstable.

Plants in the lower and coastal South sprout new roots quickly, so you can move a root-pruned plant there after a total of about eight weeks. In other locations, it is best to prune in the fall or the winter and then move the plant a full year later. In this case, it is best to mark the root ball outline with several stakes.

Making the Move

A day before the move, water the plant well. This will help the root ball stay together and will reduce the shock of transplanting. On the day of the transplanting, prepare the new location.
1. Dig up the plant along the marked root-ball line. In the case of large shrubs or trees, you may first need to dig a circular trench around the root ball (see **photograph 1** at right). The trench should extend to just below the root system. The width of the trench will vary according to the size of the plant but should be large enough to allow plenty of room to work. When the trench is deep enough all the way around, start

cutting underneath the root ball until the plant is completely free.

2. When transplanting a small shrub with a firm root ball, simply lift the shrub by the root ball (not by the trunk) and carry it. If you are moving a small tree or a large shrub or a shrub in sandy soil where the soil will easily fall away from the root ball, it is best to use a tarp to help transport the plant. Lean the plant to one side in the hole and slide the tarp under. Work the tarp underneath the root ball, shifting the plant on top of the fabric until the ball rests completely on the tarp (see **photograph 2**). Tie the tarp around the ball to hold the soil and the roots together and then move the plant to the new site. If the distance is short, slowly and gently drag the bundle across the ground. If the distance is great, use a wheelbarrow or a garden cart.

3. Measure the width and the depth of the root ball, using a shovel handle (see **photograph 3**). Then dig the new hole three times as wide as the root ball of the plant. Be sure the depth of the hole is no deeper than the height of the root ball. If the hole is too deep, the plant may not grow well.

4. Place the plant in the hole. If you used a tarp to transport it, carefully slide the plant off the tarp before setting the plant upright in the hole. Fill the hole with the soil that was removed, being careful to fill all spaces so as not to leave any air pockets. Water the plant for about four hours with a light stream from a hose (see **photograph 4**). Fill in any areas that have settled from the initial watering and place a thick layer of mulch around the plant. Water regularly during the first year until the plant becomes established in its new site.

If the plant loses all its leaves, keep watering. However, if the leaves turn brown but do not drop off, it's probably time to buy a new plant. Scratch the surface of a branch near the trunk to be sure. If you see any green at all, there's still hope—keep watering. Prune during the growing season to remove dead branches and to encourage new growth.

MOVING A TREE OR A LARGE SHRUB

1. Dig a trench wide and deep enough to provide plenty of working space.

2. Work a tarp as far under the root ball as possible. Slide the tree onto the tarp.

3. Use the shovel handle to measure the width and the depth of the root ball. Use these measurements to calculate the size of the new hole.

4. Always water a tree or a shrub immediately after transplanting.

A Special Case for Roses

With its well-deserved reputation for pricking even the casual admirer, a rosebush may not be the most desirable plant to move around. But by taking a few precautions, you can transplant it successfully while it is dormant.

The secret to success is to prepare the bush properly. But first, prepare yourself. Wear tough, prickleproof clothes and good leather gloves or elbow-length, rose-pruning gloves. Then gather the branches of the rose-bush by winding a spiral of twine around the entire plant from the bottom to the top. This keeps both branches and you from getting tangled and torn during the move.

Follow the general instructions on pages 46 and 47 to accomplish the move. Once the bush is resituated, stabilize it by staking through the center of the root ball, hammering each stake 2 feet into the ground. Water the rosebush well, add mulch, and continue to water regularly as needed.

Leave the twine around the bush throughout the winter. In early spring when buds begin to swell, remove the twine and prune any dead branches.

To prepare a rosebush for moving, bundle the branches loosely with twine. Then dig a root ball as large as you can lift. Slide it onto a burlap tarp. Move the plant as you would any other shrub.

This Pink Pet rose blooms profusely just a few months after transplanting.

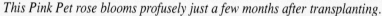

Drive a stake through the root ball to help stabilize a newly moved rosebush.

Garden Decorations

A garden is a dynamic place, constantly evolving in style and character. Inspiration is everywhere. An antique millstone becomes a contemporary fountain; a fence becomes a support for a vine-covered trellis. However, the projects in Garden Decorations aren't always about finding creative solutions to design problems. Sometimes they simply show you a way to give your garden a stylish, personal stamp.

Introduce soothing sounds and experiment with new plants by featuring water in the garden. A **Millstone Fountain** is a simple yet effective idea for putting a farm antique in a contemporary garden setting and adding complementary bog and moisture-loving plants. **Garden Pool** shows gardeners how to make a quietly beautiful focal point, using modern construction materials. **Easy Garden Fountain** transforms a weatherproof concrete container into a bubbling water feature. **Small-scale Water Garden** describes a quick-and-easy way to enjoy water gardening without going to great expense.

If you've always wanted to grow climbers, such as sweet peas, climbing roses, or honeysuckle, but you don't have any vertical supports in your garden, take a look at **Wire Trellis**. This trellis can be built in a weekend and is a great place for experimenting with lightweight vines and climbers.

The **Stick Tepee** project allows you to double the number of plants you can grow, as it gives support to climbing annual vines, such as green beans, morning glory, or mandevilla.

If you like garden sculpture, **Clay Pot Panache** will make you smile. Learn how to use terra-cotta pots to create sculptures for table-top displays and to bring the joy of the garden indoors. You can even try your hand at creating life-size clay pot "personalities."

An outdoor container-gardening project offers a different look that is fun to create. **Easy-to-Tackle Topiary** shows you how to produce the elegant look of a traditional topiary in a container by using trailing plants and sculpted forms.

Clay pots can be used to create inviting outdoor sculptures as well as charming seasonal displays.

Millstone Fountain

An old millstone finds new purpose as the focal point for this simple yet elegant fountain.

TOOLS

Copper pipe cutter

Drill with appropriate bits

Shovel

MATERIALS

Millstone

5-gallon plastic bucket

Two wading pools, one about 6' in
    diameter and the smaller one 6" to 8"
    smaller in diameter

Small submersible recirculating pump

Metal plate cut to fit hole in millstone

½" copper pipe

River rocks

Paving stones (optional)

Sand (optional)

The appeal of this fountain design is its quiet simplicity. It illustrates how to adapt a piece of farm equipment, such as a millstone, to a garden. The millstone sits atop a bucket, which rests inside plastic wading pools (a small one inside a larger one) situated below the ground. A recirculating pump creates the plume that mists over the river rocks. Bog plants around the fountain create the impression of a beautiful, natural scene just stumbled upon.

Getting Started

Dig a hole to accommodate the large wading pool. Place the large pool in the hole and backfill around it. Then place another pool that is 6 inches to 8 inches smaller in diameter into the larger one. Fill the space between the two pools with soil.

1. Drill several 1½-inch holes 1 to 2 inches below the rim of a heavy-duty 5-gallon plastic bucket. Make additional holes near the base to allow water to circulate between the bucket and the small pool. Place the bucket, which will serve as a water reservoir for the pump, in the center of the small pool.

2. Put the submersible recirculating pump in the bottom of the bucket. Thread the cord and the plug out through one of the holes and over the top of the pools toward the power source (see **Easy Garden Fountain** on page 55 for information about installing an outdoor power source). Measure the distance between the bottom of the bucket and the top of the millstone. Use a copper pipe cutter to cut a piece of ½-inch-diameter copper pipe. Bend it so that it can run from the pump to the top of the millstone. Attach the lower end of the pipe to the pump.

3. Fill the bucket with water and plug the pump into a power source to check the height of the fountain. Adjust the flow valve on the pump to fine-tune the height of the spray. Stabilize the bucket by filling the space between the bucket and the small pool with river rocks.

4. Place the millstone on the bucket, centering the hole over the copper pipe. At a sheet metal shop or a welding shop, have a metal plate cut to fit into the center of the millstone. Have the shop drill a ½-inch-diameter hole into the center of the metal plate. Thread the pipe through the hole in the metal circle and fit the circle into the center of the millstone.

Finishing

5. Pile a few little river rocks over the metal plate to conceal it, leaving the pipe unobstructed. Spread a layer of rocks over the area above the small pool. Plant bog plants or other moisture-tolerant plants in the circle of soil between the two pools. Add paving stones set in sand around the edges if desired (see **Walkways** on page 77).

6. Fill the small pool with water until the water is just below the surface of the top layer of rocks. Turn on the pump and enjoy. Some water will be lost due to evaporation, so it may be necessary to refill the pool every few days.

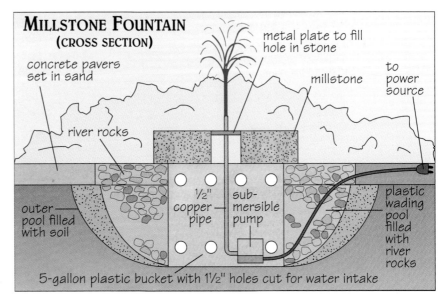

MILLSTONE FOUNTAIN
(CROSS SECTION)

metal plate to fill hole in stone

concrete pavers set in sand

millstone

to power source

river rocks

outer pool filled with soil

½" copper pipe

submersible pump

plastic wading pool filled with river rocks

5-gallon plastic bucket with 1½" holes cut for water intake

TIPS FOR SUCCESS

• Place an ad in your state farmers market consumer bulletin to locate a millstone or have an antique dealer find one for you.

• Suitable bog plants include arrowhead, bog sage, cardinal flower, Japanese iris, royal fern, and spider lily.

Garden Pool

Create a natural oasis in your garden by building a small pool.

TOOLS

Hose

Level

Shovel

Tape measure

Wheelbarrow

MATERIALS

Marking paint or sand

45-mil liner synthetic-rubber pool material

Sand

Large stone

Recirculating pump and plastic tubing (optional)

Fountain (optional)

Electrical fixtures and wiring for an outdoor power source (optional)

Nothing is as attractive as a pool of water in the garden. This project shows you how to use modern materials to build a small pool that will serve as an inviting highlight.

Choose a site that receives at least three hours of sunlight if you want to add aquatic plants to the pool. Morning sunlight is ideal, as it provides enough light to promote flowering but not so much as to encourage growth of algae in the water.

To soften the stonework around the edge of the pool, consider plantings of cardinal flower, dwarf gardenias, and ferns. For a contrast in color, try scattering white caladiums in with other plants. And to give the pool a touch of running water, rig a small fountain that complements the setting.

A sheet of 45-mil pool liner material, a recirculating water pump, and large stone are the key components of this water garden.

Getting Started

Determine where you will build your pool, keeping in mind the light requirements of the plants to be added and how the pool will fit into the rest of the garden. Then decide how large the pool should be.

1. Use a hose to define the outline of the pool in the proposed site. Adjust the placement until you are satisfied with the shape. Use marking paint, sand, or a shovel to mark the outline. Then start digging out the pool. The ideal depth of a garden pool is 18 inches.

First remove the topsoil from the entire area. Place it to one side (take care not to mix it with the subsoil that will be removed farther down). The topsoil will be used to backfill around the stone installed around the pool.

Check the edges of the hole to make sure they are level; use dirt removed from the hole to build up a dike around the low edge of the hole (see **photograph 1** on page 54).

When the hole is dug and the edge is level, you are ready to purchase the 45-mil synthetic-rubber pool liner that will form the bottom and the sides of the pool. Buy material that is resistant to ultraviolet light. (See the **box** below for an easy formula for determining how much liner to buy. Purchase a little more than you need to allow for adjustments.)

TIPS FOR SUCCESS

• Black dye formulated for pools and ponds can be added to the water to make it more reflective. (Do not use dye if you put fish in the pool.)

• Suggested aquatic plants for a water garden include anacharis, lotus, parrot's feather, pickerelweed, water lettuce, and water lily.

• Suitable bog plants include arum, arrowhead, cardinal flower, horsetail, royal fern, spider lily, and swamp iris.

• Many water and bog plants are highly invasive. Plant them in containers first and then set these into the pool.

FOUR EASY STEPS FOR ESTIMATING LINER SIZE

Step 1. Measure the length of the pool at its longest point.

Step 2. Measure the width of the pool at its widest point.

Step 3. Measure the depth of the pool at its deepest point. Double this number and then add that figure to the length measurement to determine the overall length of the pool and to the width measurement for the overall width of the pool.

Step 4. Add 1 foot to each of these overall measurements to allow for the necessary overlap. The final two sums are the required length and width of your liner.

Example: If the length of the pool is 6 feet, the width is 3 feet, and the depth is 2 feet, your liner will need to be 11 feet long (6 + [2 x 2] + 1) and 8 feet wide (3 + [2 x 2] + 1).

LINING THE POOL

1. Use a level to ensure that the edge of the pool is level.

2. Filling the pool slowly with water makes it easy to smooth out wrinkles in the liner.

3. The first set of stone overhangs the edge to hide the liner. Trim any excess liner on the outside of the stone and cover the edges with backfilled topsoil.

2. Before laying out the liner, spread a couple of inches of sand on the bottom of the hole. This will allow you to stand in the pool to work with plants without punching holes in the liner.

Once the layer of sand is in the bottom of the hole and the edge is level, carefully spread the lining across the pool. Arrange it so that an equal amount of material comes up onto the bank around the entire edge. Slowly fill the pool with water, smoothing out wrinkles on the sides of the lining material as the pool fills (see **photograph 2** at left).

3. After the pool is full, place large stone around the pool's edge. Let the stone overhang the edge of the pool by 2 or 3 inches to help hide the liner (see **photograph 3**).

Continue laying stone until you are satisfied with the look. Usually a small wall, two or three stone high, is sufficient. When all of the stone is in place, trim the excess liner and then backfill to the stone edging with the topsoil you saved from the excavation.

If you like the sound of trickling water, add a small fountain to the pool, using a recirculating pump and plastic tubing. Get recommendations regarding the selection and the installation of a pump and a fountain from someone at the same store where you purchased the liner. You will probably need a power supply for the pump. Refer to **Easy Garden Fountain** (see **step 3** on page 57) for information about installing an outdoor power source.

Finishing

With the liner installed and the stone wall constructed, you are ready to landscape. Choose plants that will thrive in the particular exposure of the setting. If you want to include live fish in the pool, consult with experts about what kinds of fish, and how many, your pool can support. There may also be other special requirements for keeping fish in a pool.

Easy Garden Fountain

You need only a weekend to construct a fountain such as this in your garden.

A fountain enhances almost any garden, from a formal planting on a grand estate to a pocket plot in a suburban front yard. The sound of splashing water or the sight of sunlight dancing on a rippling pool can add magic to the surrounding landscape.

Small submersible recirculating pumps that run on household current make it possible to easily and affordably transform a large waterproof pot into a bubbling fountain. Assembling the components yourself not only allows you to customize the design but also is less costly than buying a kit. By doing part or all of the installation yourself, you can save even more.

Getting Started

Since a fountain is likely to become the focus of the garden, select its location carefully. Consider all the angles from which it will be viewed and choose a spot where your eyes come to rest naturally. A flowerbed, a terrace, and a view framed by a kitchen window are just a few of the possibilities. The location should be level and provide a firm footing. Avoid establishing the fountain under overhanging tree limbs, unless you want to spend time fishing debris out of the water.

TOOLS

Coarse cylindrical rasp (optional)

Drill with appropriate bits (optional)

Electrical wiring tools

Level

Shovel

Wire cutters

MATERIALS

Large waterproof concrete pot

Waterproofing sealer

Miniature submersible pump with flow value

Cork

Silicone sealant

Short pressure-treated stake

Ground-default outlet

Insulated underground wiring

Junction box and outlet

¾" plastic conduit

Stone or brick (optional)

Sand (optional)

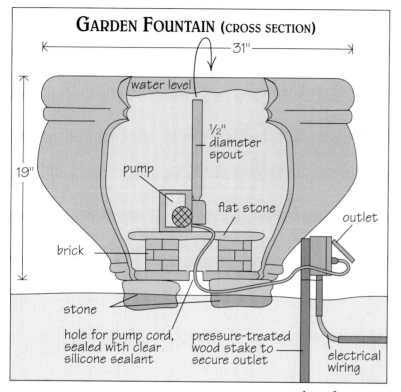

GARDEN FOUNTAIN (CROSS SECTION)

31"

19"

water level

½" diameter spout

pump

flat stone

brick

stone

outlet

hole for pump cord, sealed with clear silicone sealant

pressure-treated wood stake to secure outlet

electrical wiring

TIPS FOR SUCCESS

❖

• Add 2 tablespoons of household bleach to the water once a week to keep it free of algae.

• Do not put fish in a fountain this small.

Select a container that mirrors the style of your house and garden. Ordinary clay or concrete pots aren't suitable for a year-round fountain, since alternate freezing and thawing can cause them to crack and chip. A waterproof concrete container with a drainage hole is recommended. The 31- x 19-inch concrete pot shown at right was purchased from a concrete and statuary supplier. You can waterproof a container yourself by coating the inside with a waterproofing sealer.

Once you've chosen your pot, look for a submersible recirculating pump that will produce a spray of water of pleasing proportions. For example, a 4-foot geyser would be inappropriate for a small container, while a gentle, bubbling plume would be just right. A small pump is inexpensive, runs on household current, and uses only a few watts of electricity per day. Buy one that has an adjustable valve that regulates water output. A salesperson at a garden shop that carries water-garden supplies should be able to recommend a source for a pump and to advise you about the proper size.

Before building the fountain, try out the pump to see how it performs with your chosen pot. Temporarily plug the pot's drainage hole with a cork, fill the pot with water, and place the pump inside. Plug the pump into an extension cord that goes to a grounded electrical plug. Two ways to control the height and the force of the fountain's jet are to raise the pump within the pot and to adjust the flow valve. The valve in the pump used on page 52 adjusts water output from 30 to 83 gallons per hour. Experiment with your pump until the water bubbles without splashing.

Constructing the Fountain

When you have determined the correct position of the pump and the optimal setting of the flow valve, begin construction of the fountain. Remove the pump, empty the water, and let the pot dry out completely. If the drainage hole isn't large enough for the pump's plug to pass through, enlarge the hole, using a drill with a ⅝-inch bit. Rasp out the hole with a coarse cylindrical rasp until the plug will fit through. Place the pump in the pot and run the plug and the cord through the hole. Next, seal the hole with silicone sealant. Let the sealant dry, following the manufacturer's instructions, before putting water into the pot.

Preparing the Site

1. At the desired location, use a shovel to level an area slightly larger than the base of the pot. If the fountain is going to be surrounded by plants, elevate the pot to prevent it from being obscured by the plants (see **photograph 1** at right). Place flat stone or brick on the leveled site to raise the pot to the desired height. Arrange the stone or the brick with a gap between them to accommodate the pump's electrical cord where it comes out through the bottom of the pot.
2. Use a level to ensure that the pot is level after you have set it in place. Add sand under the stone or brick if necessary (see **photograph 2**).

Providing Electricity

3. The next step is to provide a source of electricity for the pump. If you are not familiar with the process of wiring for outdoor applications, you should hire an electrician. If you do the job yourself, you'll need to install a junction box beside the fountain and dig a 6-inch-deep trench for an electrical wire to connect to a ground-default circuit at the house. Run the electrical wire through a ¾-inch plastic conduit and place it in the trench you dug, or along a wall, to protect the wire from being cut accidentally. Follow all local codes.

Once the electrical connections are made, fill the fountain and plug the pump into the outlet.

Maintenance

Remove leaves and other debris from the water as needed. Before the first freeze, empty the fountain and pump the water out of the submersible pump so that neither will be damaged by ice.

PREPARING THE SITE

1. Raise the fountain a few inches above the ground to ensure that it is not obscured by adjacent plants.

2. Be sure the base of the fountain is level. Use sand under the supporting stone or brick, if necessary.

3. Run underground wiring through a plastic conduit. Hire an electrician if you are unfamiliar with outdoor installation procedures.

Small-scale Water Garden

This water garden can add a special touch, while introducing you to the whole world of aquatic plants.

Not every garden is blessed with a brook or a tranquil natural pool, but the charm of a water garden can be captured in any outdoor setting. Even if your garden consists of pots on a deck, you can still create a water feature in a large waterproof container. Assembling the components yourself is fun and is usually less expensive than buying a kit. A small-scale water garden such as the one at left is also a great place to experiment with aquatic plants.

Getting Started

Begin by selecting a container that suits your taste and budget as well as the final location of your water garden. Nurseries that sell water plants often have watertight containers that are made especially for water gardens. They may also be able to supply plastic liners designed to fit into wooden half-barrels if you prefer a wooden container for your aquatic plants. Large glazed ceramic cachepots and planters will also work, as long as there is no drainage hole.

You might consider unglazed terra-cotta containers as well. These pots come in a variety of styles and should be waterproofed before being used as water gardens. Buy an approved sealer from your water plant supplier or through a mail-order garden plant supplier. If the container you want to use has a drainage hole, seal the hole with a waterproof concrete patch used for mortar cracks in concrete or consult with a sales associate at a garden shop on the best material for plugging the hole (see the **photograph** at top right).

TOOLS

Paintbrush

Putty knife (optional)

Rubber gloves

MATERIALS

Large terra-cotta pot or other watertight container

Material suitable for patching drainage hole (optional)

Waterproofing sealer (optional, for terra-cotta pot)

Plastic liner (optional, for wooden half-barrel)

Dwarf arrowhead, parrot feather, sweet flag, waterclover, water hyacinth, water lilies, or other water plants

Fertilizer tablets

Mosquito preventative doughnuts (optional)

Choosing the Plants

Once you have waterproofed the container, place it in a location where it will get nearly full sunlight and then add the desired plants to it. A number of aquatic plants are well adapted to growing in containers. Hardy water lilies, with their exotic blooms and glossy foliage, are an excellent choice for the center-piece of this small water garden. Since most lilies do best when planted about 3 inches deep, you may need to place a brick under the plant to raise it to the correct height (see the **photograph** at bottom right). Other choice plants include dwarf arrowhead, parrot feather, sweet flag, waterclover, and water hyacinth.

Don't overdo it; the water lily, plus two or three other plants, will be all you need to create a satisfying composition. Place each plant, still in its small pot, in the larger container and add water.

Maintenance

Refill the container with water as needed. Feed the plants once a month with a fertilizer tablet, available where you purchased the plants. Put the tablet in each individual pot that contains a plant. Don't put any fertilizer in the water as this will promote the growth of algae.

When temperatures approach freezing, drain any terra-cotta containers and bring them inside. Successive freezing and thawing may crack or chip clay. The plants can be stored indoors in a cool area, such as an unheated basement, throughout the winter. Trim the leaves and the stems and be sure to keep the roots constantly moist.

If planted in freezeproof containers, hardy lilies may remain outside in a sheltered area, as long as the water in the container does not freeze solid to the depth of the roots.

To keep mosquitoes from breeding, put doughnut-shaped mosquito tablets in the water. These contain a bacteria that is not harmful to humans but will kill mosquito larvae.

PREPARING YOUR PLANTER

Use waterproof concrete mix to plug the drainage hole in the chosen container.

Place the plant in the dry container to gauge the depth. It may be necessary to elevate the base of the plant so that it rests at the optimum depth beneath the water.

TIPS FOR SUCCESS

- Look for a freezeproof container with no drainage hole.

- If mosquitoes become a problem, you can buy a special "doughnut" to control them.

Wire Trellis

These sweet pea vines scamper up this simple wire trellis, yielding plenty of fragrant blooms.

TOOLS

Hammer or staple gun

Pick

Shovel

Tape measure

Wire cutters

MATERIALS

Heavy-gauge galvanized or nonrusting fencing with 2" x 4" grid

Galvanized or nonrusting wire staples or large-headed nails

Marking paint (optional, for outlining trench)

Plants or seeds of lightweight vines

Most avid gardeners run out of space long before they run out of things they'd like to plant. To make the most of the space you have, consider planting vines that grow up rather than out. You can easily turn a picket fence, a storage shed, an air-conditioner screen, or the space under a window into support for fragrant sweet peas, rambling roses, or even garden beans. Just attach a simple trellis made from fencing material to the support.

Getting Started

The sweet pea trellis at left is made from lengths of heavy-gauge wire fencing with a 2- x 4-inch grid. Be sure the fencing you select is sturdy enough to support the weight of the plants you choose. If you plant annuals, you will find that the large open spaces between the wires make it easy to clean off the dead plants at the end of the season. Use galvanized or nonrusting wire fencing for your trellis to avoid staining your fence or siding.

The natural gray color of the wire fencing blends unobtrusively into the weathered tones of the picket fence. Fencing can also be spray-painted to match painted pickets or siding.

Construction

Decide where you want to build your trellis, keeping in mind that most vines flower best in full sunlight. Dig a 6-inch-deep trench for anchoring the wire fencing. Position the trench about 2 feet from the fence, the wall, or the screen that will support the top of the trellis.

Measure from the bottom of the trench to the proposed top of the trellis to determine the length to cut the fencing material. Cut one panel to the correct length. Using this panel as a guide, cut enough panels from the roll of fencing material to cover the area to be trellised.

Gently flatten the panels. Place one end of one panel in the trench and use the dirt removed from the trench to fill in around it. Attach the other end of the wire panel to the supporting structure. Continue with one wire panel at a time until the entire area is covered.

For a permanent trellis, attach the panels to the support with nonrusting wire staples every 8 to 10 inches. If the trellis is to be used for annual vines, you may decide you want to remove and store it during the off-season. In that case, use large-headed nails and simply hook the fencing over them to attach the trellis. For removal, unhook the upper end of the fencing and loosen the soil in the trench.

Finishing and Maintenance

Mulch the area between the trellis and the support in order to smother any weeds.

Prepare the soil near the base of the trellis, according to the needs of the plants. In most cases, you can use the anchoring trench as a planting area. Just be sure not to disturb the wire too much when preparing the soil and planting the seeds or the seedlings. Once the plants are established, care for them as you would in any other setting.

PLACING THE WIRE TRELLIS

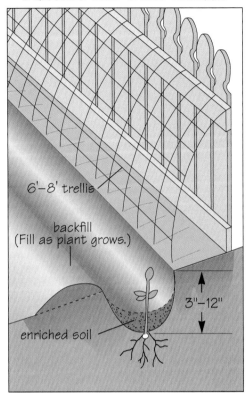

6'–8' trellis

backfill
(Fill as plant grows.)

enriched soil

3"–12"

TIPS FOR SUCCESS

- Avoid bending galvanized fencing any more than necessary, since bending can crack the finish and encourage rust.

- If your soil is very heavy with clay, you can amend it with composted cow manure and an equal amount of ground leaves or compost before planting.

Stick Tepee

TOOLS

Pruning shears

Tape measure

MATERIALS

12 freshly cut branches, each ¾"
   to 1" thick at large end

Flexible vine

Wide packaging tape

Heavy planter of appropriate size
   for site

Potting soil

Low-growing plants

Climbing plants and vines

This stick tepee, made from locally gathered natural materials,
provides a sturdy support for climbing plants and vines.

Container gardening is more fun when you have the option of growing vines and climbers, which add vertical interest to the garden. If you want to provide support for plants in a large planter, you can buy one of several types of plant supports available at garden shops. Or with just a little time and effort, you can make a stick tepee from materials in your own backyard. By doing it yourself, you will be sure that the tepee fits your planter perfectly.

Getting Started

First choose a large planter. It can be made of clay or terra-cotta, concrete, or even heavy plastic. Let the site help you determine the appropriate size of the planter. How high you make the tepee depends on the size of the planter.

The tepee shown at left can be made from freshly cut tree or shrub branches held together by woven vines. The ends of the branches (at the bottom of the tepee) are stuck into the potting soil. Climbing plants in the planter grow up the tepee.

Gathering the Natural Materials

Collect the natural materials to make the tepee; each tepee requires 12 freshly cut branches. Select straight branches that are about ¾ to 1 inch thick at the large end and are free of limbs. Place one branch in the planter and judge how tall you want your tepee to be. Remove the branch and trim all the branches to the desired length.

Next, gather the vines that will be used to weave the branches together. You will need a total of about 70 feet of flexible vine to complete a tepee designed to fit into a planter about 18 inches across. Invasive Japanese honeysuckle vine works well, as do native muscadine vines. Even kudzu vines will do the trick. Harvest vines in segments that are at least 3 feet long and ¼ inch to ½ inch thick. With the proper materials at hand, start assembling the stick tepee.

Making the Tepee

1. Turn the planter upside down so that you can use the outside of it as a form for building the tepee (see **photograph 1** at right). Use wide packaging tape to attach the branches to the outside of the planter. To space the branches equally, start by taping two branches on opposite sides of the planter. Then tape two more branches between the first two. If the bottom of the planter were the face of a clock, branches would be attached at the 12, 3, 6, and 9 o'clock positions. Now tape one branch each at the 1 and 2 o'clock positions. Continue in this manner until all 12 branches are taped in place.

2. Leave the branches at the 12, 3, 6, and 9 o'clock positions full length and trim about one foot off the upper end of the remaining eight branches (see **photograph 2**).

3. Weave a 6-inch-wide band of flexible vines between the branches, starting approximately 12 inches from the bottom of the branches (see **photograph 3**). Intertwine the vines so that the branches are pulled together to form a conical shape. Make another 6-inch-wide band of woven vines approximately 12 inches higher up the tepee.

Finishing

When the two woven bands are complete, remove the tape holding the branches to the planter. Set the tepee aside while you fill the planter with potting soil and arrange your plants in it. To provide color until other plants get established, use low-growing plants, such as marigolds, pansies, petunias, or even herbs (see **photograph 4**). Climbing plants that work well are annual vines, such as black-eyed Susan, moon-vine, and morning glory.

4. Place the tepee in the planter. Since the outside of the planter was used as the form for the structure, the tepee base will be slightly larger than the inside of the planter, producing a snug fit. (You will have to bend the base of the branches a bit to get them inside the planter.) Insert the tepee branches about 4 inches into the potting soil.

Care for the plants as you would any other potted plants. As the climbing plants start to grow, train them up the tepee, arranging them to cover open areas. Water as needed.

MAKING A STICK TEPEE

1. Use the outside of the planter as a form when constructing the stick tepee.

2. Trim eight of the branches back about 1 foot. Leave the other four full length.

3. Weave the vines between the branches.

4. Include low-growing plants to provide color until the climbing plants and vines dominate the tepee.

Clay Pot Panache

TIPS FOR SUCCESS

- Use waterproof glue for outdoor sculptures.
- For a consistent look, use new terra-cotta pots.
- Tuck in bits of moss between some of the pots to give the sculpture a weathered look.
- You can use live or silk plants in the head pot, depending on whether you plan to keep the sculpture indoors or outdoors.

Make small tabletop pot personalities and then adapt these techniques to craft large garden sculptures of your own design.

Gardeners find all sorts of ways to satisfy their creative whims, using things they have on hand—such as clay pots. Rather than letting these pots just pile up, create a "personality" to complement your garden. Start out small with 2½-inch pots. A few stacks here, a few stacks there—and you will have created a pot pal or a pot puppy.

Place these fanciful sculptures by the front door, on a garden bench, in an herb or kitchen garden, or on a tabletop as decoration for a party. They add a fun garden element to any setting.

You will need only some clay pots, florist's wire, and plaster of Paris, along with dried flowers or other accessories to give the pot pal its unique personality.

Even a pot pal gets tired after a long day in the garden.

TOOLS

Drill with appropriate bits

Hot-glue gun

Needlenose pliers

Pruning shears

Wire cutters

MATERIALS*

Fourteen 2½" terra-cotta pots

Three 4" terra-cotta pots

Plastic wrap

Florist's wire

Plaster of Paris

Old metal spoon

One 12"-long bamboo stake

Heavy-duty craft glue

Hot-glue sticks

Sheet moss

*For making a small, tabletop pot
  personality

*Not only is this pot puppy cute,
but also it won't dig up plants.*

ASSEMBLING TABLETOP POT PALS

1. To make the feet, spoon plaster into plastic-lined 2½-inch pots until they are half full.

2. Build the legs by threading three 2½-inch pots onto the florist's wire protruding from the "foot" pot.

3. Construct the torso and assemble the pots. Stand the legs side by side and bring the wires through the bottom of the 4-inch pot. Fill half the pot with plaster and secure the bamboo stake.

Getting Started

Begin by making the feet of the sculpture.

1. Line one of the 2½-inch pots with plastic wrap. Use needlenose pliers to twist a loop in a long piece of florist's wire. The loop should be a little larger than the hole in the bottom of the pot. It will keep the end of the wire from passing through the hole. Push the straight end of the wire through the plastic wrap and out the hole. Mix about a ½ cup plaster of Paris. Using an old metal spoon, fill the plastic-lined pot halfway with plaster (see **photograph 1** at left). Pull the wire loop down into the plaster until you feel it stop at the drainage hole. Set this pot aside until the plaster hardens. Repeat the process with another 2½-inch pot.

2. Now build the legs. Turn one foot pot upside down. Run the foot pot's florist's wire through the drainage hole of an upside-down 2½-inch pot. Then thread two more pots in the same way (see **photograph 2**). Repeat to form the other leg.

3. Next, begin building the torso. Turn a 4-inch pot upside down and place it on a work surface. Drill two small holes in the bottom of this pot near the outer edge of the pot and opposite each other, equally dividing the distance between the outside edge of the pot and the drainage hole. (By applying only a little bit of pressure to the drill, you won't run the risk of breaking the pot.)

Assembling the Sculpture

Referring to **photograph 3**, turn the drilled pot right side up. Stand the legs side by side on your work surface. Insert the wire from the top of each leg through one of the drilled holes in the bottom of the 4-inch pot. Using the needlenose pliers, twist the leg wires together inside the body pot. Place a piece of plastic wrap in the bottom of the pot to cover the holes.

Mix more plaster of Paris and fill this pot halfway. As the plaster is hardening, insert a bamboo stake in the middle of the pot. Be sure the stake stays straight. Once the stake is secure, slide an upside-down 4-inch pot onto the stake so that it rests on the first pot. Use a hot-glue gun to put a spot of glue on the edges of the two pots to hold them together.

4. Now you are ready to make the arms. Cut a long piece of florist's wire and twist it to make a loop in the middle. The loop should be a little bigger than the diameter of the stake. Slip the loop over the stake and thread three 2½-inch pots, one at a time, onto one end of the wire to form an arm. Use pliers to twist the end of the wire up into the bottom arm pot so that the three pots are held onto the wire (see **photograph 4** at right). If you want short arms, twist the wire tight so that the pots stack closely together. For longer arms, leave slack in the wire so that the pots do not stack inside one another so tightly.

5. Place the last 4-inch pot onto the stake (see **photograph 5**). Put a mark on the stake at about half the depth of the pot. Remove the pot and use pruning shears to cut the stake. Replace the pot and use a hot-glue gun to secure it to the pot below.

6. Also using a hot-glue gun, attach a small piece of sheet moss wherever a limb emerges from the body (see **photograph 6**). You can use live or silk plants in the head pot, depending on whether you plan to keep the sculpture indoors or outdoors.

Maintenance

If you live in a colder region of the country, you should be aware that ordinary terra-cotta pots may crack in the winter. Use a pot personality outdoors as a seasonal display or make it with weatherproof clay pots. Remember that plants in clay pots will need to be watered regularly during the summer.

Other considerations arise when this sculpture is placed indoors. If you use real plants in the head, line the pot with plastic wrap. This will prevent the pot from draining and leaking onto furniture or the floor. Do not overwater indoor plants; water only enough to dampen the soil.

4. Attach the arms. Thread three 2½-inch pots onto a long wire to form an arm.

5. To place the head, put the last 4-inch pot on top of the bamboo stake.

6. Add personality! Attach small pieces of sheet moss with a glue gun. Put live or silk plants into the head pot.

Easy-to-Tackle Topiary

After a trip to a hardware store and a plant shop, you can assemble this stately topiary in one afternoon.

TOOLS

Saber saw or coping saw

Screwdriver

Wire-cutter pliers

MATERIALS

Primary planting container

Compatible plants

4 wire baskets (2 tops, 2 bottoms)

Two ¾" hose clamps

2 coco-fiber basket liners

Potting soil

One ½" galvanized floor flange

Four ¾" galvanized wood screws

½" galvanized pipe threaded on one
   end to fit floor flange

Wire

Black spray paint

Wooden base to fit bottom of planter,
   cut from 1"-thick pressure-treated
   lumber

Controlled-release fertilizer

Finial (optional)

Silicone sealant (optional)

Training a traditional topiary takes skill, patience, and years of effort. Few of us have that kind of time today, but we still may like the look of a topiary. That's where an easy-to-tackle topiary comes in. In fact, you can assemble this elegant version in just one afternoon.

This topiary consists of two spheres held above a planter by a central pole. Each sphere is made from two wire plant baskets that are slightly smaller than the planter. One basket is attached to the pole by a hose clamp; the other is placed upside down on top of the first basket to form the sphere. This arrangement is repeated higher up the pole to create a double-ball topiary form.

Getting Started

Select a handsome pot or planter to serve as the primary planting container. It should be large enough to counterbalance the weight of the wire baskets that will be suspended above it. The intended location of the finished topiary will also influence the size of the planter, which in turn will determine the size of the wire baskets and the length of the central pole.

Use a saber saw or a coping saw to cut a wooden base to fit inside the bottom of the planter. The base should be made of pressure-treated 1-inch-thick lumber. (You may want to get the base cut at the store where you purchase the wood.)

Attach a ½-inch galvanized floor flange (available in the plumbing section of hardware stores) to the center of the wooden base, using ¾-inch galvanized wood screws. Then decide how long to make the central pole of the topiary, keeping in mind that it should be in proportion to the size of the planter. Buy ½-inch galvanized pipe to use as the pole; one end of the pipe should be threaded to fit the floor flange. (A sales assistant at your local hardware store can cut the pipe to the desired length and then thread the end.) Screw the threaded end of the pipe into the floor flange. Tighten as much as you can by hand (don't use a wrench).

Making the Topiary

You are now ready to construct the topiary from the wire baskets.

1. Attach a ¾-inch hose clamp to each of two baskets. To do so, thread a piece of wire through the clamp and around the spokes of the basket, using wire-cutter pliers to twist the ends of the wire (see the **photograph** on page 70). Twist just until the wire is snug. Do this in four positions, equally spaced around the clamp.

2. Slip one of these baskets (with the hose clamp) down over the pipe. The basket should be in an upright position. When you have it positioned where you want it, tighten the hose clamp around the pipe to hold the basket in place. Put the remaining half of the basket (without a clamp) upside down on the pipe. Repeat the procedure to form the second sphere.

With a little time and a few tools, common materials can be transformed into a topiary.

Secure the hose clamp to the basket with wire. When the clamp is tightened around the pipe, the basket will be held in place.

3. Spray-paint the entire assembly black. When it is dry, place the wooden base in the bottom of the planter and fill the planter with potting soil. Firm the soil well around the wooden base.

4. Slide the top basket of the lower sphere up the pipe so that you can prepare the lower basket of the sphere for planting. You can fashion a small hook from a short piece of wire to hold the basket up while you work on the lower half. Line the basket with a coco-fiber basket liner and fill the lined basket with potting soil that you have prepared by mixing in controlled-release fertilizer. Follow the fertilizer manufacturer's instructions to mix the potting soil. To prepare the upper sphere for planting, remove the top basket and place the coco-fiber liner and the potting soil in the lower basket of that sphere.

Planting the Topiary

Plant each of the prepared baskets with the plants you have chosen. Include plants of varying leaf shapes and forms in your topiary.

5. To give your topiary an established look right from the start, use some plants that already have long tendrils. Make it easy to change plants for different seasons and for varied color accents by leaving some plants in their original containers and then placing the whole pots into the soil. To make the spheres look fuller, slit the liner and insert plants from the bottom and the sides. Once all the plants are installed, water thoroughly.

6. Slide the top basket of the lower sphere back in place and replace the top basket of the upper sphere.

Maintenance

Frequently check the soil in the planter and the baskets, and water as needed. Prune the plants to keep the topiary's form.

TIPS FOR SUCCESS

- Do not use plywood for the wood base as it won't hold up under wet conditions.

- Suggested foliage plants for shade include ajuga, coleus, ferns, hosta, miniature ivy, and wintercreeper.

- Suggested foliage plants for sun include coleus (sun-tolerant types), dusty miller, geranium, ivy, liriope, Madagascar periwinkle, oregano, parsley, sage, and thyme.

Paving and Masonry

Outdoor living areas can be greatly enhanced by the addition of walkways, edgings, and walls. Although you may prefer to purchase prefabricated materials or to have a professional install these brick, stone, and concrete additions, the four projects detailed here will give you ideas for building attractive features in your landscape.

In the **Stepping-stones** section, you will find an easy way to create unique concrete pavers for your garden path. These instructions offer two options for artistic expression, but feel free to use your imagination to fashion other types of designs. Making these stepping-stones can be fun for the whole family, since everyone—children, adults, and even pets—can be tempted to make a mark in wet concrete.

Walkways offers a mortarless way to dry-lay paving material to form a path. Using this method, gardeners with no construction experience can create handsome hard surfaces wherever they need them.

Edgings are important design elements that save you time on upkeep and make your garden look more attractive. Try your hand at working with brick and mortar or construct a natural-looking stone edging with no mortar.

The **Stone Wall** project shows you how to give structure to a slope. The same idea can also be applied to featuring plantings and building raised beds or walls around trees, opening up new possibilities for accent areas.

You can expand or reduce the scope of any of these projects to suit your individual needs. Just be sure to measure carefully and to adjust the materials list accordingly. Personnel at most home-design stores can help you accurately assess the materials you will need for your particular project.

These concrete stepping-stones are practical and attractive and lasting reminders of youthful fun.

Stepping-stones

TOOLS

Chisel

Concrete joint tool

Concrete trowel

Drill with appropriate bits

Handsaw

Level

Ruler or tape measure

Scrape board to use as screed

Screwdriver

Shovel

Wheelbarrow

Gardeners create paths out of a wide variety of materials, but few walkways make as individual a statement as one formed with stepping-stones. This stepping-stone project gives you the ability to personalize ones for your garden. Try pressing leaves from trees in your garden into the fresh concrete or use ferns to achieve a fossil-like look. Invite some of your favorite young gardeners to make their mark on history; imprints of little hands and feet add a whimsical touch to the garden and are a constant reminder of the good time had in making them.

You can cast a series of stepping-stones from a single wooden form.

WOOD

Pieces	Quantity	Thickness	Size	Notes
Base	1	½"	48" x 48"	Use exterior-grade plywood.
Base supports	3	1½"	3½" x 48"	Cut from a 12'-long 2 x 4.
Frame sides	2	¾"	3½" x 48"	Cut from an 8'-long 1 x 4.
Frame sides	2	¾"	3½" x 49½"	Cut from an 8'-long 1 x 4.
Divider	2	¾"	1½" x 48"	Cut from an 8'-long 1 x 2.

OTHER MATERIALS

Portland cement and sand or nonaggregate concrete mix

Finely crushed gravel or stone

1¼" wood screws

4-penny nails

Form, linseed, or vegetable oil

Wood stain or latex paint (optional, for finishing)

Leaves (optional, for pressing into the fresh concrete)

TIPS FOR SUCCESS

- If you need a number of stepping-stones, speed up production by constructing several pouring forms.

- Use a paintbrush to apply diluted green or brown wood stain or latex paint to the impressions on a finished stepping-stone to emphasize the leaves.

- When installing the stepping-stones, be sure that they are placed on solid, flat ground. Otherwise, they may crack or break. Prepare ahead by spreading 1 to 2 inches of sand or finely crushed gravel or stone to form a stabilizing bed for the stepping-stones.

Getting Started

These stepping-stones are made by pouring freshly mixed concrete (a purchased mix such as Quikrete® is easiest) into a form. Level and smooth the concrete and then press leaves, hands, feet, or other items into the wet concrete to make an imprint. This wooden form is constructed so that four stones can be made with each pouring. Your path design dictates how many stones you will need. Add just one or two handprint or footprint stones as accents in an existing path or use several to lead to a children's play area or to a swimming pool. You may want to create a whole walkway of foliage imprints in a shade garden.

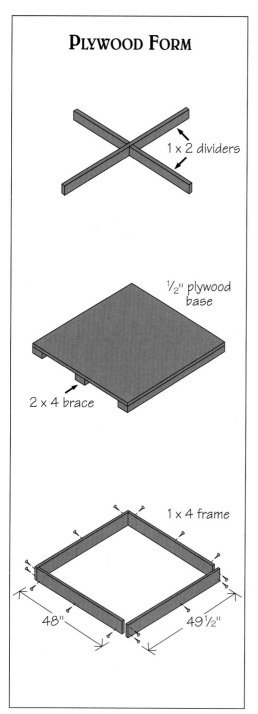

PLYWOOD FORM

1 x 2 dividers

½" plywood base

2 x 4 brace

1 x 4 frame

48"

49½"

Construction of the Form

You can build a single form and make the stones one at a time, but the job will go faster if you use a four-sectioned form. This multipad form is made up of three components: a plywood base, a wooden frame, and a wooden divider. The plywood base is supported by three 2 x 4s, and the frame slips down over the base. This creates a square box that is 1½ inches deep. A wooden divider is placed on the plywood inside the frame to form four compartments, each just under 2 feet square.

Plywood Base

The base is made of ½-inch exterior-grade plywood. You will need a 48-inch square of plywood, which is a half sheet. (Many lumberyards and home-supply stores sell half sheets or will cut one for you.)
1. Cut three 48-inch-long pieces of 2 x 4 as supports for the base. Use 4-penny nails to attach the 2 x 4s to the plywood, placing one piece along each of the two opposite edges and the third piece in the middle. Position the 2 x 4s flat side down. Make sure that no part of the 2 x 4s extends beyond the edge of the plywood; any protrusions will get in the way when you slip the wooden frame over the base.

Wooden Frame

2. To make the frame, cut two 1 x 4s to the exact length of two opposite sides of the plywood. (If the plywood was cut accurately, this measurement should be 48 inches. For a precise measurement for each board, align the boards to be cut with the plywood and mark them.) Then cut two 1 x 4s, each 1½ inches longer than the boards in the first set. Place the pieces along the corresponding sides of the plywood; the boards should be flush at the corners. Using two screws at each corner, screw the pieces together to form a square box. (Always drill a pilot hole for each screw first to prevent splitting.)

Wooden Divider

3. Now make a divider from two 48-inch-long pieces of 1 x 2 lumber. Trim the pieces to match the actual inside measurements of the frame. This divider will fit inside the frame and will be attached to the base so that four stepping-stones can be made at a time.

To allow the two pieces to overlap each other at the center, you need to prepare a lap joint (see the **illustration** on page 92). One half of the thickness is removed from each piece so that the pieces will be flush when joined.

To make a lap joint, first mark the area to be removed. Use a pencil to mark where the two pieces cross to define four equal squares on the plywood. Cut along the lines with a handsaw (one with fine teeth, such as a backsaw, is best). Cut a little less than halfway through each piece. Use a chisel to remove the wood between the saw cuts. When you have removed about half the thickness of each piece, check the fit of the joint. Remove a little more wood at a time, as necessary, until the two pieces fit together with their edges flush at the joint. When satisfied with the fit, use a screw to secure the joint. Drill a pilot hole first to avoid splitting the wood. Then attach the divider to the base with screws. Make sure that the ends of the divider are even with the edges of the base so that the frame can slip down over the base.

4. After the divider is attached to the base, fit the frame over the base. Fasten the frame to the base, using a screw in each corner.

5. Place the finished form on a flat, level surface. Brush oil liberally on all surfaces that will come in contact with the concrete. The oil will help you get the concrete stones out of the form and will aid in cleaning the form for the next pouring.

Pouring the Concrete

6. To mix the concrete, combine one part portland cement to three parts sand. To make four stepping-stones, load five shovelfuls of cement and 15 shovelfuls of sand into a wheelbarrow and mix thoroughly. (A nonaggregate concrete mix may be used instead if you don't want to buy the sand and the cement separately.)

Add water to the mixture a little at a time to avoid making the concrete overly runny (too much water will weaken the concrete). The ready-to-pour concrete should be thoroughly wet but thick.

7. Shovel or trowel the concrete into each quadrant of the form, paying particular attention to filling the corners. Use the point of your concrete trowel to cut vertically at the corners to eliminate air pockets. Smooth the concrete, using the trowel. Then finish leveling it with a *screed* (a scrap of lumber a few inches longer than the width of the form; see the **illustrations** on page 81), working back and forth across the form. Add or remove concrete in front of the screed as needed. Once the concrete is level across each quadrant, draw a concrete joint tool, a trowel, or a screwdriver at an angle along the edges of the stepping-stones to chamfer them (see **photograph 1** on page 76). This will help prevent chipping along the edges of the stepping-stones.

MIXING CONCRETE

To prepare the concrete for your stepping-stones, you can buy prepared nonaggregate concrete mix that just requires water, or you can start with cement and sand and mix your own. The route you take will depend on how many stepping-stones you want to make. The prepared mix is more expensive but more convenient to use. Be sure to read carefully the manufacturer's directions and all warnings.

To make your own concrete mix, buy portland cement and sand. Use a ratio of one part cement to three parts sand. Mix these two ingredients thoroughly in a wheelbarrow before adding water. When they are well mixed, add water slowly, stirring well after each addition. Only add the minimum amount of water needed to make the concrete workable. Too much water will make the concrete weak. Properly prepared concrete is thick enough to be mixed on a flat surface, such as a sidewalk. The same consistency is the target if using a prepared mix.

When finished mixing, use running water to clean up the tools immediately.

MAKING A STEPPING-STONE

1. Draw a concrete joint tool, a trowel, or a screwdriver at an angle along the edges of the stepping-stone to chamfer (bevel) them.

2. Pick several fresh leaves, such as these hydrangea leaves. Press the leaves into the surface of the concrete.

3. Peel the leaves from the concrete and let the stepping-stone harden completely.

Finishing

8. For each stepping-stone, pick several fresh leaves in a variety of sizes and shapes (see **photograph 2** at left). Press the leaves into the surface of the concrete so that they make a clear impression; then carefully peel them off (see **photograph 3**). Or press hands or feet into the concrete and use a stick to write the corresponding person's name and the date. You might even be able to coax a cat or a dog into lending a paw to the effort.

9. Let the stepping-stones cure at least three days, spraying them lightly with water each day so that the concrete cures slowly. Or place plastic over the form after spraying the stones so that they do not dry too quickly. Since concrete gains strength as it ages, the slower the stepping-stones cure, the stronger they will be. On the fourth day, unscrew the form and take it apart gently, letting the sides fall away. (Numbering the sides of the form beforehand will help you put them back together again easily when you make more stones.) Remove the divider and lift out your custom-made stepping-stones. Rub any rough edges with a brick to smooth them.

Let the stepping-stones cure at least another two days before setting them in place.

The beauty of leaves can be accented with wood stain or with latex paint.

Walkways

Every yard and garden needs a walkway. But a walkway is not just for walking: it is part of the overall design of the homescape. Creating a brick-and-mortar surface for a high-traffic area requires a lot of strength and skill. Fortunately, there is an easy alternative. A dry-laid walkway is attractive and may be as firm, stable, and durable as any set in mortar. In addition, you can easily adjust the pattern of a dry-laid walkway or completely remove the paving, if needed or desired.

The dry-laid method of paving involves these simple steps: building a frame, leveling and packing a bed of sand or fine gravel in the frame, setting the pavers in place, and sweeping sand into the joints.

Several paving materials can be dry-laid successfully. Stone may be used, but the most common material is brick or concrete pavers. Precast concrete pavers feature regular shapes and flat bottoms, which make them easy to install. And since the pavers come in a variety of sizes and colors, you will be able to select just the right style to enhance the existing feel and look of the chosen area. (See page 81 for tips on selecting pavers.)

Converting an old concrete walkway and a brick stoop (left) into a new dry-laid walkway with a landing (above) made a dramatic difference in the appearance of this home.

TOOLS

Brick saw (optional)

Broad-bladed cold chisel
(optional)

Broom

Drill with appropriate bits

Hammer

Handsaw

Level or straight 2 x 4

Mason's hammer (optional)

Rake

Rubber mallet

Safety glasses (optional)

Shovel

String or marking paint

Tape measure

MATERIALS

Treated 2 x 4s, 2 x 6s, or 6 x 6s;
landscape timbers; or metal
edging

Treated 1 x 4s (optional, for
curves for frame)

Stakes (treated 2 x 4s or 1 x 4s)

Galvanized nails

Sand

Finely crushed stone or gravel

Pavers

12"-square board and 4 x 4 about
4' long

2 x 4 or 1 x 4 for screed

Getting Started

Whichever material and pattern you select, the process of building a dry-laid walkway is the same. The most important step for ensuring a durable final product is to lay a level, packed foundation that allows for proper drainage.

The dry-laid method requires a border to keep the foundation and the paving in place. Various materials can be used for the border, including 2 x 4s or 2 x 6s on edge, 6 x 6s, and metal edging. The top of the border should be flush with the top of the finished paved surface, so it's usually necessary to set a portion of the material forming the border into the ground. For this reason, when using wood, be sure to use pressure-treated wood that is suitable for ground contact. (The treatment tag on the wood should show a preservation retention level of at least 0.40.)

The dimensions of the border depend on the size of the pavers you plan to use. To limit having to cut any of the pavers, make the length and the width of the border multiples of the paver size. For example, the inside dimensions of a border prepared for 16-inch-square pavers should be a multiple of 16 inches in both directions. Unlike mortar-set pavers, no space is left between dry-set pavers, but some room must be allowed for any irregularities in the pavers. A good rule of thumb is to add 1 inch to the length and to the width for every 8 feet of the border.

If you plan to use brick as a paving material, you may have to cut some of the brick, regardless of the dimensions of the border. To cut brick, you will need to rent a brick saw. Or if you have only a few to cut, try the old-fashioned method: Use a broad-bladed cold chisel, a mason's hammer, and safety glasses to protect your eyes from any flying chips. Set a marked brick on a flat surface and position the

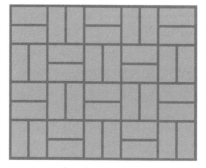

Basket Weave

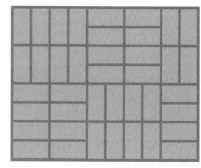

Double Basket Weave

broad-bladed cold chisel along the intended cut. Position the chisel so that the bevel is facing away from the side of the brick that is to be used. Use light hammer taps on the chisel to cut a small groove across all four sides of the brick. For the final cut, make a sharp blow with the hammer along the groove on one of the broad surfaces of the brick. Use the chisel end of the mason's hammer to chip away any rough edges.

Installing the Borders

Once you have decided on the dimensions of your border, you are ready to start.

1. Mark exactly where the borders will be installed, using string or marking paint. Following the outline, dig a trench along each side to set the edging deeply enough into the ground so that the top of each border will be flush with the finished paved surface. (In most cases this will be about even with the surface of the ground.) Check to make sure the trenches are level.

2. Work on each trench in sections. Place a piece of the border material into each trench as you work, checking the fit. You may have to dig out some or refill a little to get the depth where it should be.

3. When you are satisfied with the fit of the border material in the trenches, it is time to secure the material in place. The method for doing this depends on the type of material you are using. Metal edging usually has slots spaced along the back to receive steel stakes driven into the ground about 6 feet apart. A 6 x 6 piece of lumber can be secured by a ⅜-inch steel reinforcement bar (called #3 rebar). With the 6 x 6 in place, drill ⅜-inch holes through the 6 x 6 about every 6 feet. Then pound an 18-inch piece of the rebar into the ground through each hole. The 2 x 4s or 2 x 6s are nailed to wooden

Determine where the new walkway will go. Measure carefully to avoid having to cut pavers to fit.

Interlocking brick pavers lend themselves to various designs. Choose a pattern that best complements the surroundings.

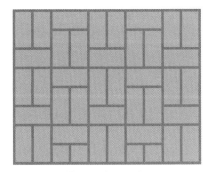

Half Basket Weave

Herringbone

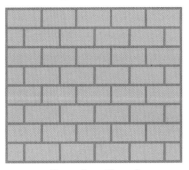

Running Bond

CREATING A WALKWAY

1. Use a board as a screed to level the sand, creating an even surface at a height that will set the pavers slightly higher than the frame.

2. Check your work regularly to keep everything straight and level.

3. Sweep sand into the joints to complete the job.

stakes spaced about 6 feet apart that are driven into the ground along the back of the boards. Saw the top of the stakes off flush with the board.

4. To make curves in the paving border, use a saw to score the pressure-treated 1 x 4s with ¼- to ⅜-inch-deep cuts, spaced ¼ inch apart. The cuts will allow the wood to bend. Or you can try metal edging. Curved borders may need to be staked more frequently than every 6 feet.

Leveling the Foundation

5. Once the border is in place, remove any grass, weeds, roots, or shrubs that are inside the frame. Using a rake, level the soil to a depth of 2 inches greater than the thickness of the paving material you plan to use. Add a layer of sand or finely crushed stone, wet it down, and then tamp it firmly. (You can make a suitable tamp from a 12-inch-square board nailed to the bottom of a 4 x 4 post.) Repeat this procedure until the sand bed is just over 2 inches deep. Finally, use a screed to level the sand to the desired depth (see **photograph 1** at left and the **illustrations** at right).

6. To use the screed, start at one end of the frame and slowly slide the screed back and forth until the sand along it is even. Fill in any depressions and pack any soft spots. Tamp one final time before installing the pavers. Compacting the sand will help keep pavers from settling later.

Laying the Pavers

7. Begin installing the pavers in one corner. Make sure the pavers rest snugly against each other. Don't slide them into place, however, or you'll disturb the bed of sand or finely crushed stone. As you place each paver, tap it tightly into place with a rubber mallet. Use a level to make sure the tops of all the pavers are even (see **photograph 2**). Don't worry if any pavers extend slightly above the frame; they will settle over time.

8. Once the pavers are in place, sweep dry sand over the surface of the walkway, filling in all the joints (see **photograph 3**). Wet the walkway down with a fine spray of water and sweep more dry sand into joints until all the cracks and the joints are filled.

If any pavers settle too much, remove the problem pavers one at a time and replenish the sand or the crushed stone beneath. An occasional refilling in the joints will help keep the pavers tight. Simply shovel more sand on the walk's surface and sweep it into any cracks.

TIPS FOR SUCCESS

- A 40-inch-wide walk allows enough room for two people to walk comfortably side by side.
- Use marking paint (available at paint stores) to outline your walk. Some regular spray-paint cans won't work when you hold them upside down to paint an outline on the ground.
- To build a screed, cut a straight board—such as a 1 x 4 or a 2 x 4—so that it fits inside the frame with 2 or 3 inches of play on each side. Attach a 12-inch-long piece of scrap lumber to each end so that the long board will drop into the frame at a depth just slightly less than the thickness of the pavers.

Screed

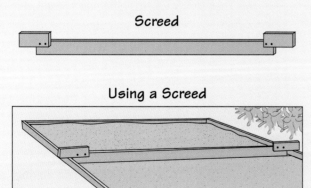

Using a Screed

CHOOSING PAVING MATERIAL

Choose a type and a color of paver that will coordinate with and complement your surroundings. If using new brick, be sure to get SW (severe weathering) grade. The standard 4- x 8-inch size is the easiest to work with. Select brick that is at least 1-inch thick. To calculate the quantity needed, figure on five brick per square foot of paved surface.

Some gardeners like the look of old brick that has been salvaged. However, used brick is often softer and, therefore, more prone to cracking or chipping. It can also vary in thickness from brick to brick.

Interlocking brick pavers are easier to work with than ordinary brick. They have a lip on the bottom edge that helps lock them together.

Precast concrete pavers come in several sizes, but the most common is a 16-inch square that is 2 inches thick. These pavers are considerably larger than brick; therefore, fewer are needed, and laying them goes somewhat faster.

Natural stone can be used, but it is a little harder to work with because of the irregular shapes.

Edgings

You know where the lawn is supposed to end and where the flowerbed begins—but your grass never seems to. A permanent edging can solve the problem of keeping grass from creeping where it's not wanted. Two options for permanent edgings are brick or stone. In addition to being practical, brick or stone edgings are attractive and require little upkeep.

Installing mortared brick edgings can be more expensive and complicated than stone, but brick offers several advantages. The course of brick that lies level with the ground provides a track for the wheels of your lawnmower, while the brick laid on their sides forms a low lip that will help keep mulch inside planting beds. A third alternative is to stand the brick on end to make an even higher lip, enabling you to raise the level of the beds if you wish.

In some situations, however, brick may be too formal. Or perhaps the cost and the effort of installation may deter you. If either of these is the case, try using stone. Flagstone pieces, about 12 inches long and 6 to 8 inches wide, are perfect for setting an edge. Also, they are easy to install and lend a rustic look to any setting. Because flagstone is not cheap, you may want to recycle stone from another project. Or visit a construction site and ask if they have any loose stone available.

Brick edging keeps the lawn tidy, holds mulch in place, and makes mowing easier.

Getting Started

First, decide which material is right for your landscape. If the edging is for the front of a brick home in a subdivision, brick could be just the thing. On the other hand, a free-form flowerbed in the backyard may look a lot better edged with casual material, such as stone, than with more predictable brick.

Next, figure the amount needed of your chosen material. If you have some brick on hand, lay them out and measure how many it takes to cover a few feet. Calculate a brick-per-foot average and multiply that figure by the number of feet of edging you wish to build. Make this calculation once for the brick that will be laid side to side and again for the brick that will be placed end to end. When you lay the brick out, remember to space them about a ½ inch apart to allow for the mortar that will be placed between each brick. If you do not have any brick available, a brick-supply house will be able to help you figure how many brick you need (if you know the length of the area to be edged).

Calculating the quantity of stone needed can be more difficult, since the material is irregular in every dimension. A stone supplier can help estimate the amount needed if you describe the project and indicate how long the edging is to be, as well as what type of stone you wish to use. A visit to the stone supplier may be necessary to select from the various types of stone.

Edging with Mortared Brick

1. Even if you decide to hire a mason to lay the brick, you can still save money by preparing the trench where the brick will be set. Use a hose to outline the area where the edging will be constructed to help you visualize where it should be. When satisfied, mark the outline, using a shovel or a pick, by spraying with marking paint, or by pouring a line of sand. Then dig a trench to a depth of about twice the thickness of a brick and a little wider than the finished edging will be.
2. Now it is time to mix the mortar, following the instructions on the bag. Put a bed of wet mortar along approximately 2 feet of the trench. Make the mortar bed thick enough that the top of the course of brick will be at the desired level. If you are inexperienced at laying brick, start working in the most inconspicuous spot of the area to be edged. (Don't be timid about pulling everything out and redoing it until you get it right. It is easy to scrape the wet mortar off the brick with the trowel and to reapply fresh mortar.)

TOOLS

Level

Mattock or shovel and pick

Mortar joint tool

Trowel

Wooden or rubber mallet

MATERIALS

Marking paint or sand (optional)

For brick edging
Amount, size, and color of brick to suit your project

Prepared mortar mix or portland cement and sand

Water supply for mixing mortar

For stone edging
Amount of stone to suit your project

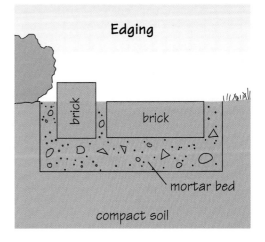

Edging

brick

brick

mortar bed

compact soil

TIPS FOR SUCCESS

Part of the secret to laying brick properly is using mortar of the right consistency. If the mortar is too thick or too runny, it will not stay on the edges of the brick. Getting it just right takes a bit of trial and error.

Add water a little at a time to the mortar and mix it in thoroughly. When all of the cement in the mixture is wet, try setting a few brick. If the mortar is crumbly and won't stick to the brick, add a small amount of water, mix well, and try again.

If the mixture is too runny, add a little of the dry mortar mix and blend it in well.

Even when you get the consistency right, remember that the situation is only temporary. The mortar is drying out as you work, so you will have to constantly adjust the consistency by adding water and blending well with a trowel.

3. Use the trowel to swipe a layer of mortar on the top and the ends of a brick and gently place it on top of the mortar. Repeat with the next brick, placing it so that there is a mortar joint between the two brick about a ½ inch thick. Set both the flat-placed brick and the brick on their side (or stood on end) as you go. Tap each brick with the handle of the trowel to make sure it is well seated in the mortar bed and use a level to make sure the edges of the brick are even.

4. When you near the end of the mortar bed, place more mortar in the trench and continue as described above.

5. As the mortar in the joints between the brick begins to firm up, use a mortar joint tool to smooth the joints and to give a professional look to your edging.

Edging with Stone

Edging with stone can be a much simpler process than edging with brick and mortar.

Use a mattock or a pick and a shovel to make a trench as described for the brick edging. The depth will depend on the size of the stone and how high you want the edging to be. Place a stone in the trench and select another one that will fit nicely next to it. Try to match shapes and colors of stone as you proceed. After a few stone are in place, backfill around the sides with soil removed from the trench. Use a wooden or rubber mallet to tamp this soil firmly in place.

Set stone loosely in a hand-dug trench to be sure that they are level. Adjust trench, if necessary.

Place pieces of stone about 12 inches long in the adjusted trench; pack soil firmly around each stone.

Stone Wall

A hand-stacked stone wall gives structure to a hillside and serves as a visual anchor for garden plantings.

In many gardens a stacked stone wall provides a handsome, natural-looking framework for perennials, herbs, and ground covers and gives the garden a focal point in the winter. It's simple to design a stone wall that fits in with existing trees and other garden features. Although it may take you some time to construct this wall, you can easily correct any mistakes since no mortar is used. Work at your own pace and learn as you go. When you get the hang of it, use the same technique to build raised beds to feature trees and flowers.

TOOLS

Hose or string

Leather gloves

Level

Pick

Shovel

Wheelbarrow

MATERIALS

Quarried native sandstone or other locally available flat stones (The quantity depends on the height and the length of the wall.)

Sand (optional)

Topsoil (optional)

Getting Started

First, determine exactly where you want to build the wall. A hose or some string works well to outline and to help you visualize the shape of the wall. Remember to include gentle curves to accommodate existing features, such as trees, shrubs, or garden trails. Gradually taper each end into the slope. When laying the wall, keep the height to about 3 feet or less; otherwise, the wall will need a concrete footing or foundation.

Once you are satisfied with the location and the layout, mark the outline made by the hose or the string. This can be done with a shovel or a pick, or by pouring a line of sand.

Then measure the length of the wall and estimate how tall it will be at its highest point. If you used a hose or some string to outline the wall, it is easy to measure the length, even though the wall has lots of curves. Simply mark the end point and stretch

Use a hose or a piece of string to outline the shape of your wall.

the hose or the string out straight and measure to the mark. The length and the height of the wall will help the stone supplier figure how much stone you will need to buy.

The supplier can also help you choose which type of stone to buy for your project. Irregularly shaped quarried stone (called rubble) looks more natural than cut stone and costs less. It is sold by the ton—which sounds like a lot but actually isn't—and the supplier will deliver.

Construction

A sturdy wall needs a solid footing. The depth of the footing will depend on the desired height of the wall and the type of soil you are working in. For a short wall with a height of approximately 2 feet, a 6- to 8-inch-deep trench should be sufficient. Make sure the trench is level, though the depth at each end may gradually decrease as it turns into the slope (see **photograph 1** at right). When the trench is finished, tamp the soil to firm it and then set the first course of stone. Select large flat stone to give the wall a sturdy base. Try to keep all the stone level. You may have to try several different stone to get just the right fit.

Add the next course, staggering the stone so that one joint is not on top of another; continue placing stone, backfilling as you work up (see **photographs 2** and **3** at right). Tamp the soil each time you backfill to reduce the settling of soil behind the wall.

As you place each course of stone, keep in mind that the wall should lean back into the slope approximately 1 inch for every foot of height in order to provide stability. Individual stone should also lean back so that the front of each stone is slightly higher than the back. If a particularly irregular stone totters on the stone below it, wedge a thin stone between the two to act as a shim (see **photograph 4** on page 88).

Check periodically with a level to make sure that the wall is even. Make any necessary adjustments

Building a Stone Wall

1. Dig a flat, level trench that follows the curves of your design.

2. Backfill with soil as each course is added. Tamp the soil behind the wall to reduce settling later.

3. Stagger the stone so that the joints between the stone in one course don't line up with the joints in the course below.

BUILDING A STONE WALL (CONTINUED)

4. Wedge a small, thin stone between unstable ones to prevent wobbling.

5. Use large, attractive stone in the visible final course. Check to make sure that the wall is level.

as you lay each course, carefully selecting and trying out stone of various sizes and shapes to help keep the wall level.

Reserve some of the biggest and best-looking stone for the top course, which will be the most visible (see **photograph 5** at left). These stone should be consistent in thickness, in width, and in length.

Finishing

Backfill behind the finished wall. You may have to import soil to completely fill the area. Tamp the soil well but don't overly compact it, as this will put undue stress on the wall and could cause drainage problems. Landscape the area as desired. Many stone walls in older gardens are adorned with cascading plants, such as pinks, thrift, or verbena; others are draped with ivy or prostrate rosemary. Consider a planting of perennials above the wall and annuals in front of it to provide seasonal color.

Or you can simply scatter a mixture of easy-to-grow seeds over the soil. This can result in a most productive cutting garden, such as the one pictured on page 85. The mixture of bachelor's buttons, cosmos, and zinnias offers a bright spectrum of color and blooms on long stems throughout the summer.

TIPS FOR SUCCESS

- The delivery charge for stone is usually per trip rather than per ton. Be sure you get enough so that you don't end up having a small load delivered to finish the job. You can always use any leftover stone for small projects, such as steps or paths.

- Select small stone to fill gaps between irregular edges and to help make the last course level.

Hammer and Nails

Gardeners are a creative lot who easily switch from one set of tools to another. From a window box to a rough-hewn fence, there are all sorts of projects in this chapter that call for a hammer and nails, along with other tools of the woodworking trade. These projects can make your garden more enjoyable and attractive, whether you do them yourself or collaborate with someone who has construction experience.

Accenting a garden with special plants, containers, and other features makes this space more personal—and is also a lot of fun. To enliven a blank wall, create a canvas for flowering vines with **Trellis.**

Porch sitting is a Southern tradition. The porch offers an excellent vantage point from which to enjoy the sights, the scents, and the sounds of the garden. But if your porch is a little too public, make it more private by following the instructions for the **Lattice Screen** project. In **Outdoor Screening** you discover how to hide a functional area of the garden from visitors.

A fence frames the garden and gives it a feeling of intimacy, in addition to providing a screen. This type of structure also creates a natural backdrop for tall, showy plants, such as foxglove or sunflowers, flowering vines, and climbing roses. The **Rustic Fence** features a handsome fence that suits a variety of garden styles.

Unadorned windows can be spruced up with either an **Outdoor Plant Shelf** that will hold potted plants or a handmade **Window Box**. A **Planter Box** makes it possible for a deck or a porch to be decorated with a seasonal spot of color. And a **Mailbox** adds a grace note to a streetscape. All of these will add personality to your landscape.

So when you grab your planting trowel, watering bucket, and controlled-release fertilizer on a Saturday morning, remember to look around your yard and see what a hammer-and-nails project could do for your garden. Sometimes the simple addition of an accessory, a bed, or a vertical structure is all it takes to give a garden a special sense of place.

Select plants for your window box as carefully as you do for your garden. These impatiens do extremely well in a location shaded from the afternoon sun.

Trellis

Vines are the jewelry that accent a garden. They take our eyes from the ground into the treetops, over doorways, and along fences. Vines also soften and beautify buildings. If you don't have anywhere to grow vines, this easy-to-make trellis provides just the place. It's sturdier than most store-bought trellises and is less expensive than many in garden catalogs. Pick a corner of the house or a spot near a door where you could use a vertical accent and seasonal color. Some vines like full sunlight, while others grow in shade. Bear this in mind when selecting a location for your trellis.

The trellis attaches to brackets with wood screws rather than with nails, allowing easy removal of the trellis when it is time to paint the area behind it. The brackets hold the trellis several inches from the wall, giving the vine space to grow and you room to prune. The space created also adds the illusion of depth and creates interesting shadows. A low-voltage lighting fixture can be positioned below the trellis to create dramatic effects at night.

This trellis is ideal for climbing or twining vines, such as flowering clematis, Carolina jessamine, or Confederate jasmine. For lustrous evergreen foliage, try planting smilax. The trellis will also work for an annual vine such as morning glory or for mandevilla, which is a tropical vine. These can be trained in the summer to grow over evergreen vines, covering them with seasonal blooms. Or let a climbing rose cover the trellis—a charming touch.

Vines need to be lightly tied to the trellis or trained to weave in and out of the squares. Use copper wire, soft twine, or rope to train vines and to tie branches loosely.

This simple trellis frames a vine that enlivens the white background with rich green foliage.

Getting Started

Since the trellis will be outside and exposed to the elements, it should be made of a rot-resistant wood, such as redwood, cypress, or No. 1 grade pressure-treated pine. The 2 x 2s will be joined to form 12-inch open squares. At the top, both vertical and horizontal rails extend 4 inches beyond the square in each direction to create open corners, giving an old-fashioned, picture-frame effect. The remaining horizontal rungs are joined to the inside of the vertical rails. The lowest horizontal rung is positioned 18 inches from the ground. Brackets attach the completed trellis to the wall.

Construction

The first thing to do is determine how tall the trellis will be. The one pictured is 6 feet 5½ inches, including the four 1½-inch 2 x 2s forming the four 12-inch squares. The bottom rung is 18 inches from the ground, and there is a 4-inch extension from the fifth 1½-inch rung.

Rails and Rungs

1. When the overall height is determined, cut the two vertical rails to that length. Then position them side by side on a flat work surface.

TOOLS
Backsaw (or other fine-toothed saw)
Chisel
Drill with appropriate bits
Hammer
Handsaw or circular saw
Level
Paintbrush
Screwdriver
Square
Table saw or radial saw
Tape measure

WOOD

Pieces	Quantity	Size	Length	Notes
Rails	2	2 x 2	6' 5½"	Adjust length if desired.
Rungs	4	2 x 2	12"	Miter ends.
Top rung	1	2 x 2	23"	
Brackets	4	2 x 2	15"	May be cut longer, if desired.

OTHER MATERIALS

Exterior oil-based primer (optional)

Exterior latex paint or stain and water-treatment sealer

1½" nails or wood screws

Low-voltage light (optional)

Toggle bolts

Exterior wood glue

Metal brackets (optional)

1" nails

LAP JOINT

The lap joints may be cut on a table saw or a radial arm saw. If you don't own either saw, you may have the joints cut at a cabinet shop or by a friend who has one of these saws.

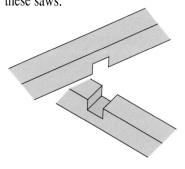

TIPS FOR SUCCESS

• If you don't mind the 2 x 2 bracket extending past the vertical pieces, cut it at least 17½ inches long. The bracket will then be able to catch a stud on each end, and you will not have to be concerned with toggle bolts. To soften the look of the exposed bracket ends, cut the ends at an angle.

• You can easily adjust the size of the trellis to fit your chosen spot. Make it a few inches shorter by positioning the bottom rung closer than 18 inches to the bottom of the rails. If you make the trellis taller, do so in 12-inch increments.

Measure 18 inches from one end of each board and mark a line across both pieces, using a pencil and a square. Mark an X beside each line (to the side that is greater than 18 inches). Next, mark a line and an X at 31½ inches, 45 inches, 58½ inches, and 72 inches on each board. These lines indicate where to position each horizontal rung.

2. Cut four 12-inch-long pieces and one 23-inch-long piece of 2 x 2. The 23-inch piece will be the top horizontal rung, which will extend past the vertical rails by 4 inches on each side.

Lap Joints

3. To allow for the top horizontal rung to extend past the two vertical rails, prepare a lap joint (see the **illustration** at left). One-half of the thickness of both the horizontal and vertical pieces is removed so that the pieces will be flush when joined. A critical first step is to mark the material to be removed. Spread the rails apart, using two of the four rungs as spacers. Lay the 23-inch rung across the rails where it will be attached. Mark with a sharp pencil where the rails and the rung cross.

Using a handsaw (one with fine teeth, such as a backsaw, is best), cut each piece along the line a little less than halfway through the thickness of the wood. Remove the waste with a chisel. When you get close to the halfway point on each piece, start checking the fit. Remove a little at a time from the pieces, as necessary, until you are satisfied with the fit on both the joints.

Placing the Rungs

4. Predrill small holes through the vertical rails where the horizontal rungs are to be attached. Place a little exterior wood glue on both surfaces and nail or screw on the first four horizontal rungs. Then fit the lap-jointed top horizontal rung in place, applying glue first. Tack this piece down with a 1-inch nail at each joint.

Mounting the Brackets

5. While the glue is setting on the trellis, prepare the mounting brackets. One option is to use the same 2 x 2 material from the trellis; that is particularly desirable if you plan to attach the trellis to a wooden wall. If you are attaching it to a masonry wall, you may need to use metal brackets. Someone at your local hardware store should be able to recommend suitable brackets, as well as an appropriate way to fasten them to the wall.

If you have decided to use the same 2 x 2 material, cut four pieces 15 inches long. Measure and mark a horizontal line on the wall 61 inches from the ground, using a level. Attach one of the 15-inch-long 2 x 2s to the wall (with the top edge on the line). If you are attaching the bracket to a wooden wall, you may be able to nail one end of the 2 x 2 to a wall stud. (Predrill the hole in the 2 x 2 and use a 16-penny galvanized casing nail.) The 15-inch-long piece is not long enough to catch two studs, however, so the other end will need to be attached with a toggle bolt. In that case, prepare the toggle bolt hole before attaching the piece to the stud. Again, a salesperson at your hardware store should be able to help you select the proper toggle bolt and instruct you how to use it.

Painting, Staining, or Sealing

6. Stain or paint the trellis and the brackets before the trellis is installed. If painting, use an exterior oil-based primer, followed by a quality exterior latex paint. In areas of high humidity, have someone at the paint store mix an additive to combat mildew into the paint when the color is blended for you.

If you wish to leave your trellis natural, apply a water-treatment sealer to avoid cracking and checking of the wood. If you want to stain it, apply the stain and then apply the water-treatment sealer after the stain has dried thoroughly.

Attaching to the Wall

7. Once you have the first piece of the top bracket attached, measure 40½ inches from the top of it. Use a level to mark a straight and level line at this point, marking the top of the bottom bracket.

8. You can also use the level to make sure the brackets are aligned vertically. Attach a 2 x 2 bracket to the wall as described above. Now screw the other 2 x 2s on top of the attached bracket pieces. This will cause the trellis to be held a total of 3 inches from the wall. The brackets should be positioned so that the trellis is supported about 1 inch off the ground and the brackets line up with the first and fourth rungs.

Finishing

9. When the finish is dry, attach the trellis to the brackets, using wood screws. Predrill the holes in the trellis to avoid cracking.

ALTERNATIVE DESIGNS

If the lap joints seem like too much fuss and bother, forego the extensions on the top horizontal piece. Just nail or screw it in place as you do the four other horizontal pieces.

On the other hand, if the lap joints seem like a fun challenge, consider preparing lap joints for all five of the rungs.

If you think you would like an overhang on all of the rungs but do not wish to make so many lap joints, redesign the trellis to accommodate butt joints. Simply nail or screw the horizontal rungs on top of the vertical rails, rather than chiseling out wood to make them flush. The look is not as finished, but it may suit your particular needs.

Lattice Screen

One of the best places to wind down at the end of the day is the porch, especially in the South. Sometimes, though, you want to relax in privacy, and passing traffic can be bothersome. This attractive lattice screen lets in the breeze and permits you to enjoy the natural ambience while blocking you from the sight of passersby. A similar screen could be used anywhere in the garden that you want a sense of seclusion or need a backdrop for vines or climbing roses.

Getting Started

The screen is based on a prefabricated lattice panel of pressure-treated pine. It is secured by 1 x 2 framing strips in a frame built from 2 x 4s. Lath strips and 2 x 2s make up the trim. The finished screen is primed and painted to match the surrounding decor.

Each porch is different, so your screen will have to be custom-built. When determining the position and the size of the screen, keep in mind that lattice comes in 2 x 8 or 4 x 8 panels. It can be cut, but working with entire panels is easier and faster.

Construction

Using a tape measure to help you visualize the dimensions, determine where the panel should be located and how large it should be.

Basic Frame

1. Measure from the floor to the ceiling to determine the length required for the two 2 x 4s. Cut these pieces and check the fit. If the floor has settled, the measurements may vary slightly between the two pieces. Label the pieces as to which one goes where. Take the difference into account when attaching the top and bottom 2 x 4s. The frame has to be square for the lattice to fit properly.

This easy-to-build lattice screen provides privacy while adding beauty.

WOOD

Pieces	Quantity	Size	Length	Notes
Uprights	2	2 x 4	Floor to ceiling	
Top and bottom	2	2 x 4	48"	Adjust length to width of lattice panel.
Framing strips	4	1 x 2	8'	Miter ends.
Framing strips	4	1 x 2	4'	Miter ends.
Lath strips	2	1½"	Floor to ceiling	
Trim	4	2 x 2		Varies with project.
Lattice panels		2 x 8 or 4 x 8		Varies with project.

OTHER MATERIALS

16-penny galvanized casing nails

6-penny galvanized casing nails

1" wire brads

2" wood screws

2" metal L or corner braces

Masonry anchors

Exterior oil-based primer

Exterior latex paint

TOOLS

Drill with appropriate bits

Hammer

Handsaw or circular saw

Nail set

Screwdriver

Tape measure

2. Decide where the bottom supporting 2 x 4 should be positioned. Ideally, you want to split the distance that the 8-foot panel doesn't cover between the top and the bottom. For example, if the distance from the floor to the ceiling is 9 feet 6 inches, subtract 8 feet from this for the panel, plus 3 inches as the combined thickness of the top and bottom 2 x 4s. This leaves a space of 1 foot 3 inches to be divided between the top and the bottom. Therefore, the top and bottom 2 x 4s will be positioned 7½ inches from the ends of the upright 2 x 4s. If the distance from the floor to the ceiling is greater than 10 feet, position the bottom 2 x 4 approximately 12 inches from the bottom end of the uprights. A space greater than 12 inches will look out of proportion.

3. Attach the bottom 2 x 4 at the proper distance from the ends of the upright 2 x 4s. Measure 8 feet from this 2 x 4 and attach the top 2 x 4. Be sure you have an 8-foot space between the top and bottom 2 x 4s. Use 16-penny galvanized casing nails to attach these pieces, predrilling the holes first to avoid splitting.

TIP FOR SUCCESS

❖

After the lattice panel is set in the frame, it may be a bit difficult to drive the nails to attach the framing strips that hold the panel in place. The panel tends to interfere with the hammer stroke. Eliminate part of this problem by using a nail set to drive a nail into a predrilled hole. The nail set will allow you a cleaner hammer stroke (and help you to avoid striking the lattice).

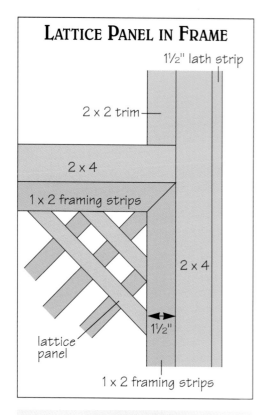

LATTICE PANEL IN FRAME

1½" lath strip

2 x 2 trim

2 x 4

1 x 2 framing strips

2 x 4

1½"

lattice panel

1 x 2 framing strips

ALTERNATIVE CONSTRUCTION

If you have a table saw and a dado blade, you can modify the construction. Cut a dado into all the 2 x 4 pieces. The dado should be centered on the 2 x 4s, wide enough to receive the lattice panel, and ¼ inch to ⅜ inch deep. Attach the bottom 2 x 4 to the two upright 2 x 4s and then slip the lattice panel in place. When the top 2 x 4 is attached, the panel is secured in the 2 x 4 frame. Lath strips can be substituted for the 1 x 2 framing strips. The 2 x 2s placed on the inside of the upright pieces hide the dado that extends past the panel. The overall look is basically the same.

Place the Lattice Panel

4. Now, you have the basic frame built. The lattice panel will be held in this frame by two 1 x 2s (one on each side of the lattice). Predrill pilot holes. Use 6-penny galvanized casing nails to attach one set of 1 x 2s to the top and bottom 2 x 4s and to the upright 2 x 4s. Position the 1 x 2s so that the lattice panel is centered on the 2 x 4s. The 1 x 2s should be nailed in place on edge (see the **illustration** at left). Predrill all the nail holes in the 1 x 2s to avoid splitting and to make driving the nails easier.

5. When the first set of 1 x 2s is attached, set the lattice panel in place. Finish making the frame by nailing in the second set of 1 x 2s.

6. A lath strip (attached with 1-inch wire brads) centered along the outside of each upright 2 x 4 adds a finishing touch. Also, 2 x 2s can be added to the inside of the upright 2 x 4s between the ends and the horizontal 2 x 4s. Center them on the 2 x 4s. Use 2-inch wood screws to attach them.

Finishing

7. To finish, paint the completed panel so that it matches the porch. First, prime it with an oil-based exterior primer and then paint it with an exterior latex paint. For areas of high humidity, include an additive to combat mildew when your paint is mixed to the desired color.

Lattice is difficult to paint with a brush or a roller. Spraying is the best way to get good coverage.

Installation

8. When the paint is dry, it is time to install the new screen. Be sure to have at least one helper; the structure is not superheavy, but it is awkward. Position the screen as planned. If installing it onto wood, use 16-penny galvanized casing nails to toenail the upright 2 x 4s to the floor and to the ceiling. If the floor is concrete, stone, or some other masonry, you will probably need to use 2-inch metal L or corner braces. These are easily attached to the 2 x 4 with wood screws. To attach them to the masonry, first install a masonry anchor that is recommended by someone at your local hardware store.

Additional Trim

For a more formal look, quarter round can be installed against the 2 x 4s and the framing strips. This can be done on each side or just on the side that needs dressing up.

Outdoor Screening

Install lattice screening to hide unsightly necessities and to beautify an area.

Nearly every home has an air-conditioning unit, a hose, a garbage can depository, blank spaces under a deck, or some other necessary-but-not-very-attractive area that the homeowner would prefer to hide from public view. Shrubbery or small trees can be planted to screen the eyesore, but plants take years to be mature enough to do the job right. This project offers an outdoor screen that not only conceals the uglies but also gives you a vertical structure for growing beautiful climbing plants.

This backyard was filled with an assortment of shrubs, an air-conditioning unit, and various garden tools.

TOOLS

Circular saw	Level
Hammer	Posthole digger
Hand plane	Square

WOOD

Pressure-treated Southern pine (quantities determined by your screen design):

Heavy-duty lattice paneling

4 x 4 posts (treated for ground contact)

2 x 4s

2 x 6s

Prerouted U-channel strips

OTHER MATERIALS

16-penny galvanized deck nails

1" galvanized finishing nails

8-penny galvanized finishing nails

3" galvanized gate hinges

1 adjustable-tension metal brace (for each gate)

1 gate latch (optional, for each gate)

2" galvanized gate hinges

Gravel

Sandpaper

Concrete mix

String

Commercial deck wash

Exterior oil wood stain

Plants

Getting Started

Feel free to modify the ideas presented here to fit your needs. The screen should be constructed of materials that match the house, the deck, or other structure that is already present. Lattice was used in our model to coordinate with the existing deck, and access was provided by gates at each end of the screen.

Lattice was also installed beneath the deck for a miniscreen that hides the original unattractive black hole. All the wood should be pressure-treated pine. In addition, purchase a heavy-duty type lattice panel and 4 x 4 posts that are rated suitable for ground contact.

Constructing the Screen

Determine where you want to construct the screen. Keep in mind that access to the area is important and plan accordingly. Once you have decided where to put the screen, make a scale drawing of it (see the **box** on page 101). This will help you calculate materials needed and where to place the posts. Remember that the prefabricated lattice panels come in 2 x 8 or 4 x 8 sheets, so don't space the posts more than 8 feet apart.

With the design in hand, prepare the site. Remove any shrubs, trees, and flowers that are in the chosen area. Relocate them to a new spot in the garden or use them later to landscape around the screen.

Setting the Posts

1. With the proper materials on hand, you are ready to begin construction. The first step is to determine where to position the 4 x 4 end posts that hold the lattice. Then dig a hole approximately 18 inches deep for each post and fill each hole with a layer of gravel. Stand a post in each hole; make sure each post is level. Fill the holes with concrete and tamp the concrete around each post. Use a level to make sure the posts are vertical. The erected posts should be taller than the final height of the screen. They will be cut to the correct height later.

2. After the two end posts are set, erect the intermediate posts. First, stretch a string between the two end posts to align where the intermediate posts should go. Measure along the string according to your plan and mark the positions of each of the intermediate posts. When you have all the positions for the intermediate posts marked, dig a hole at each post position. Dig the hole deep enough so that the 4 x 4 pressure-treated posts can be set at least one foot into the ground. Place a layer of gravel into each hole before standing the posts. Pour in the concrete, making sure that the posts are vertical. Next, set the posts for the ends of the screen. These posts will be at right angles to the end posts and will support the lattice or the gate at each end of the screen. Set them as you did the intermediate posts (see **photograph 1**).

Cutting the Posts

3. The next step is to cut the posts to the proper height. In determining the height for the screen, keep in mind the height of what you are trying to hide. At the same time, remember that the screen should not be so high as to interfere with objects that should not be obscured (such as windows). Measure the desired height from the ground on one of the posts; cut the post to that height. Use a straight 2 x 4 and a level to mark that same level on the remaining posts. Use a circular saw to cut all the posts to the proper height.

Making the Basic Frame

4. To make the base for the screen, lay a 2 x 4 close to the ground between each post. Level the 2 x 4s and attach them to the posts, using 16-penny galvanized deck nails.

Placing the Lattice Panels

5. Prepare the lattice that will sit on top of the base 2 x 4s and between each post. The lattice will be framed by prerouted U-channel strips. Measure between two posts and cut the lattice panel to fit

1. Set posts 1 foot deep in the gravel; pour in the concrete and make sure that the posts are vertical. Cut them to the proper height later.

2. After attaching the bottom 2 x 4 rail to the posts, frame the lattice panel with prerouted U-channel strips. This frame-within-a-frame design strengthens the fence.

3. Attach the 2 x 6 top rails after the panels are in place. Keep the top rails flush along the entire length of the fence.

INSTALLING THE SCREEN (CONTINUED)

4. A single 35-inch gate provides easy access behind the screen.

5. Hinges on the small panels beneath the deck allow the panels to swing up for subfloor access.

between these posts. Remember that the U-channel strips will add to the width of the lattice panel, so determine how much it adds and adjust the measurement for the lattice panel accordingly.

6. The same principle applies in cutting the panel to the right height. Measure from the top of the base 2 x 4 to the top of the post. Cut the lattice panel to fit this space, again allowing for the space that the U-channel strips will add to the panel height. When the lattice panel is cut to the proper height and width, cut the U-channel strips to fit the panel. Attach them with 1-inch galvanized finishing nails. The frame-within-a-frame design strengthens the fence (see **photograph 2** on page 99).

7. Now place the panel assembly between the posts and let it rest on the base 2 x 4. Center the assembly on the posts and the 2 x 4 , using 8-penny galvanized finishing nails. Repeat this procedure for each space between posts, leaving an open area for a gate. Then attach the 2 x 6 top rails, using 16-penny galvanized deck nails (see **photograph 3** on page 99). Each rail nails on top of the 4 x 4 posts and overhangs the sides of the posts by 1 inch on each side. Cut the rails to length so that they are flush with the end posts.

Building the Gate

8. If your design calls for a gate, it is time to build it. Use 2 x 4s to make the bottom and the sides of the gate frame and a 2 x 6 for the top of the frame. Build the gate to match the height of the screen. The width should be about ⅜ inch less than the opening the gate will fit into. Cut a piece of lattice panel, frame it with U-channel strips and install it in the gate as you did with the panels between the posts. Install an adjustable-tension metal brace to give the gate support and to keep it square. Use 3-inch galvanized gate hinges to mount the gate. On the post opposite the hinges, attach a 2 x 4 to act as a gate stop. You can also add a gate latch to lock the gate if desired (see **photograph 4** at left).

Covering Beneath the Deck

9. You gain two things by adding lattice panels to the space between the deck floor and the ground. It will make the deck look better and will visually tie the screen to the deck. Prepare lattice panels framed in U-channel strips to fit the space. Use hinges to attach some panels to provide access to the area. Attach the panels with 2-inch galvanized gate hinges so that they swing up (see **photograph 5** at left).

Or use the space beneath the deck for a play area or for storage. Adding a bed of gravel or mulch nuggets makes the space usable without interrupting drainage. Apply an herbicide to any remaining grass or ground cover before pouring the gravel or the nuggets.

If your deck is too low for people to fit under, it may be just the right height for a pet (see **photograph** on page 4). The dog's owner boxed in a spot under his deck; a wooden awning keeps it shady and cool. When your deck is too low for even a dog to squeeze beneath, enclose it to conceal gaping spaces. Nail 1-inch-thick lumber horizontally to the posts for an attractive alternative to lattice trimwork. Leave small spaces between lumber to allow air to circulate.

Finishing

10. If you wish to soften the edge on the 2 x 6 rail on top of the screen, use a hand plane to round the top edges a bit. Then smooth them with sandpaper.

11. Let all the new wood dry for two to three weeks before bleaching and staining. This process will give your screen a finished look and help it blend with the existing decking. Use a commercial deck wash to clean both the new screen and the old deck, following manufacturer's instructions. Then apply an exterior oil wood stain to the screen and the deck.

12. To complete the job, landscape around the new screen. Use some of the plants that you removed from the site or design a new planting. Plant climbing roses or vines or design a shrub-and-flower border, placing taller plants in the back.

MAKING A SCALE DRAWING

To draw your plan to scale, you will need a sketch that shows the measurement of your screen. You will also require a tape measure, a sketch pad, a pencil, and a helper if the screen is to be longer than 5 or 6 feet.

Measure the distance you want the screen to cover, being sure to include corner posts and the gate area. Sketch these dimensions on paper, noting the exact dimensions of all the elements.

You are now ready to complete your drawing to scale. Using graph paper, redraw your sketch (a common scale is 1 inch to 10 feet). Measure and draw with a pencil the lines taken from your sketch. You may need to change some dimensions, so have an eraser handy. Once the graph drawing is completed to your satisfaction, you are ready to begin calculating the materials you will need to finish the project.

TIPS FOR SUCCESS

- If hiding an air-conditioning unit, be sure to allow enough space between the unit and the screen for workers to make repairs to the unit when it is necessary.

- Use a handheld sprayer to apply the commercial deck wash.

Rustic Fence

A vertical pole fence may provide just the right kind of rustic screen for your garden. A string of tiny white lights (under the edge of the cap) makes a nice finishing touch.

TIPS FOR SUCCESS

❖

• Space the 4 x 4 posts evenly along the length of the fence. If the total length is 12 feet, set the posts 6 feet apart.

• When possible, cut the poles ahead of time to give them a chance to season. If using green poles, pull the bailing wire between them tightly so that they won't rattle loosely in the fence frame when they dry and shrink.

Gardens often call for a fence to set off one area from another or to shield something, such as a utility area, from view. In casual settings, a white picket fence or a wrought iron fence may look too formal. And the traditional split-rail fence does not provide a good screen and may be too country looking for some gardens.

Here's a new idea for a rustic fence that screens effectively and works with almost any garden style. It pairs smooth-cut lumber with rough-wood poles for a handsome look. You may use cedar (as shown) or experiment with another material, such as bamboo or cypress. (Just be sure to use wood that will withstand the elements.) Leave the bark on or remove it to change the effect.

Getting Started

The fence is constructed in sections. Vertical 4 x 4 posts (suitable for ground contact) provide the main structural support; an elevated base keeps the poles off the ground and helps hold them in place. Horizontal 1 x 4 rails at the top and near the bottom contain the poles and provide rigidity. Bailing wire woven through the poles near the bottom helps keep the poles together tightly; a recessed 1 x 4 does the same at the top. A 2 x 8 cap above the 4 x 4s provides the final touch.

Finishing

1. Finishing usually comes last, but with this project, it's easier to do before the fence is assembled. You can paint the posts and the rails with exterior latex paint, using an exterior oil-based primer first. Then when you complete the project, touch up any areas soiled during construction. Stain is another finishing option for the lumber. Be sure to leave the poles rough and unfinished.

Construction

First, decide where you want to build the fence. Next, measure the total length and calculate the amount of materials needed. Allow for a 4 x 4 post every 8 feet or less.

Setting the Posts

2. Determine where the posts will be placed and dig a hole approximately 18 inches deep for each post. Put a layer of gravel in each hole. Stand a post in each hole and then fill in the holes with concrete, checking frequently with a level to make certain that all the posts are vertical. Tamp the concrete into the hole around each post.

It's a good idea to set the two end posts first and to stretch a string between them to align the posts in between. Let the concrete set for at least a day before continuing work on the project.

Building the Base

3. Next, build the base. You will need to choose between a low concrete wall or a stone wall. With the poles in place, it is easy to build a low concrete wall. Use 8-penny nails to attach level 1 x 4 boards from post to post on both sides along the ground so that a box is formed. Fill this box with concrete and let it dry for two full days; then remove the 1 x 4 boards. A simple stone wall can be built by stacking flat stone two or three high between the posts.

TOOLS

Circular saw

Drill with appropriate bits

Hammer

Level

Paintbrush

Posthole digger

Shovel

String

Tape measure

WOOD

1 x 4s—5 for each section

4 x 4 posts suitable for ground contact— enough for one every 8' or less and as long as desired fence height (plus any portion that will be buried)

Rough poles—no larger than 3½" in diameter with length cut to fit between base and upper rails (less ¾")

2 x 8—enough to cap entire fence (Allow approximately a 1-inch overhang on each end.)

OTHER MATERIALS

8-penny nails

Bailing wire

Eyebolt screws (one for each post)

Base material

Exterior oil-based primer (optional)

Stain or exterior latex paint (optional)

Gravel

Concrete

Flat stone (if building a stone wall base)

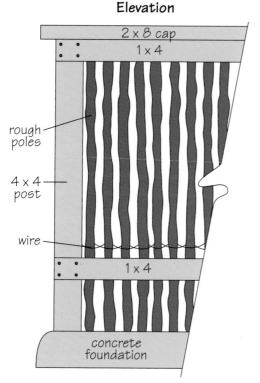

Elevation

2 x 8 cap
1 x 4
rough poles
4 x 4 post
wire
1 x 4
concrete foundation

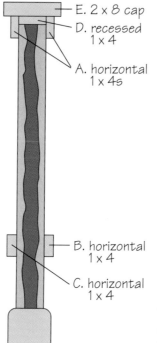

Cross Section

E. 2 x 8 cap
D. recessed 1 x 4
A. horizontal 1 x 4s
B. horizontal 1 x 4
C. horizontal 1 x 4

MEASURING ROUGH POLES

When trying to cut the poles to the proper length, you may discover that the irregular shape of each pole makes getting an accurate measurement difficult. An easily constructed measuring jig will help. Start with a 2 x 6 about a foot longer than the desired length of the poles. Nail a scrap board across the end of the 2 x 6 so that the end of the pole will butt up against this scrap board. Mark the desired length of the poles on the 2 x 6. Lay the pole on the 2 x 6 with the end against the scrap board. Cut the pole where it crosses the line on the 2 x 6.

Setting the Framework

4. After the posts and the base have been completed, attach the horizontal 1 x 4s to the top of the posts on both the front and the back (**part A** in the **cross-section illustration**). Flush the top of the 1 x 4s with the top of the posts. Nail a horizontal 1 x 4 rail to the posts about 8 inches from the bottom on the back of the fence (**part B**). Make sure the boards are horizontal. You may have to trim the posts to the height of the shortest one so that the top horizontal boards are level.

Installing the Poles

5. The next step is to select poles that are no greater than 3½ inches in diameter so that they will fit into the space defined by the horizontal 1 x 4 rails. Measure the distance from the top of the posts to the base. Cut the poles ¾ inch shorter than this measurement. This allows a 1 x 4 to be placed on top of the poles and still be flush with the top of the upper rails.

6. Working on one section at a time, stand the poles in place; attach a fourth horizontal 1 x 4 to the posts (**part C**) to serve as the front rail. It should be at the same level as the back rail (**part B**). Fit the recessed 1 x 4 (**part D**) across the tops of the poles and between the upper 1 x 4 rails. Nail through this recessed 1 x 4 into the tops of the rough poles. (Before nailing, position the tops of the poles so that each pole is vertical.) Cap the fence with a 2 x 8 laid flat and nailed into the tops of the 4 x 4 posts (**part E**). The 2 x 8 will overhang the sides of the top rails by about 1 inch. Allow the same overhang on the ends.

Securing the Poles

7. The final step in the construction is to secure the lower portion of the poles with bailing wire. The wire should be installed either above or below the lower rails. Drill a small hole in the back of each post and screw a small eyebolt into each hole. Thread bailing wire through the eyes and weave it through the poles (see the **elevation illustration** above).

Outdoor Plant Shelf

This window shelf puts a garden of potted mums at your fingertips.

Imagine colorful annuals, aromatic herbs, and fragrant miniature roses growing right at your fingertips—it's possible with this handy window shelf. The shelf makes it so easy to change out plants—and to take care of them. This shelf would also be a natural addition for a window from which you regularly watch birds from the spring to the fall. You may want to locate the shelf outside a kitchen window and stock it with herbs. Or put it on a home office window so that you can enjoy the change of seasons with appropriate flowers, such as potted mums in the fall.

Getting Started

The shelf is made from a 2 x 10 bordered on three sides by 1 x 3s. The 1 x 3s are trimmed with 1-inch quarter round attached to the top edges to create a ¾-inch lip around the shelf. (If it is difficult to find pressure-treated quarter round, use untreated wood and be sure to prime and to paint it well.) The ends of the 1 x 3s and the quarter round are mitered for a professional look. The shelf is supported by wooden decorative brackets, which attach to the studs of the outer wall frame. The shelf is attached to the brackets at a slight slope so that water runs toward drainage holes drilled near the outer edge (see the **illustration** at right).

All of the material should be pressure-treated pine if available. The brackets are partially protected from the weather by the shelf above them, so it is not as critical that they be rot resistant.

Construction

1. Start by determining how long your window shelf should be and where it should be positioned on the window. Measure the distance the shelf will span and cut a 2 x 10 to 1½ inches less than the measurement. (The 1½ inches will be taken up by the 1 x 3s attached to each end of the shelf.)

TOOLS

Backsaw

Drill with appropriate bits

Hammer

Miter box

Nail set

Screwdriver

Square

Table saw (optional)

Tape measure

WOOD

Pieces	Quantity	Size	Length	Notes
Shelf	1	2 x 10	According to situation	
1 x 3 trim	1	1 x 3	Same as shelf	Miter corners.
1 x 3 trim	2	1 x 3	9¼"	Miter corners.
Quarter round	1	1"	Same as shelf	Miter corners.
Quarter round	2	1"	9¼"	Miter corners.
Brackets	2	Varies	Varies	

OTHER MATERIALS

Exterior wood glue

Galvanized wood screws 1" and 1½" longer than thickness of brackets

Wood filler

Exterior oil-based primer

Exterior latex paint

4-penny finishing nails

¼" flat washers

Sandpaper

Caulk

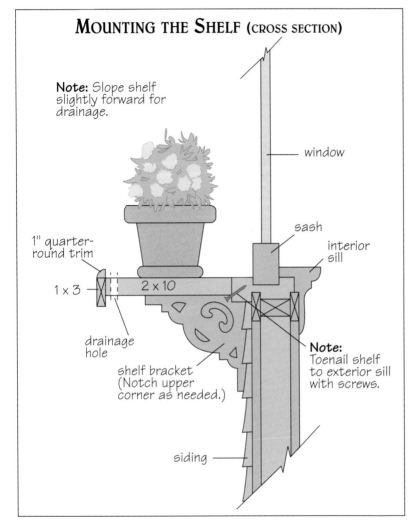

MOUNTING THE SHELF (CROSS SECTION)

Note: Slope shelf slightly forward for drainage.

window

1" quarter-round trim

1 x 3

2 x 10

sash

interior sill

drainage hole

shelf bracket (Notch upper corner as needed.)

Note: Toenail shelf to exterior sill with screws.

siding

Building the Shelf

2. Along one long edge of the 2 x 10, drill ¼-inch drainage holes, ¼ inch from the edge and 5 inches apart. Cut 1 x 3s to fit three sides of the 2 x 10. (Get someone at a lumberyard to produce a nonstandard 1 x 3 by ripping a 1 x 4. Or do it yourself with a table saw.) Use a miter box and a backsaw to miter the corners. Attach these 1 x 3s to the 2 x 10, using 4-penny finishing nails and exterior wood glue on both surfaces. Align the top edge of the 1 x 3s with the top of the 2 x 10. Attach the long 1 x 3 to the 2 x 10 edge with the drainage holes. Predrill the holes. Cut 1-inch quarter round to fit on top of the 1 x 3s. Miter the corners. Use exterior wood glue on both surfaces and attach quarter round with 4-penny finishing nails.

TIPS FOR SUCCESS

- Attach the quarter round to a 1 x 3 long enough to furnish the three pieces needed. Use exterior wood glue on both surfaces and secure them with 4-penny nails. Do not drive the nails in all the way. Measure and cut the pieces needed for the three sides of the 2 x 10. (If a nail is positioned where you want to cut, pull it out with pliers.) This assures that the 1 x 3 and the quarter round are cut to the same length and that the miters fit snugly.

- To install the shelf on a brick wall, set the shelf below the brick lip of the windowsill and attach it with expansion bolts. Someone at your hardware store should be able to help you choose the correct fasteners.

- Ask the sales associate to cut 2 x 10s to 1½ inches less than the measurement.

- Prime all the pieces of the shelf, including the brackets, before assembling. If using pressure-treated pine, allow it to weather three to four weeks before priming and painting.

- Decorative brackets may be purchased for $20 or less.

If you own a router, you can use it with a roundover bit to rout the top edge of the lip instead of using quarter round. In this case, use 1 x 4s rather than 1 x 3s and attach them so that the top edges extend above the 2 x 10 by a ¾ inch. Once they are attached, run the router around the edges to round them. Smooth any irregularities with sandpaper. (A 1 x 4 is a ¼ inch wider than a 1 x 3 with a quarter round attached—3½ inches versus 3¼ inches.)

Attaching the Brackets

3. With the shelf complete, you are ready to prepare the decorative brackets. If the sill is thicker than the 2 x 10, it may be necessary to cut a notch out of the bracket to allow room for the sill (see the **illustration** on page 107). To determine how large the notch should be, hold a piece of scrap 2 x 10 up to the sill (keep the top edges flush) and measure from the bottom of the sill to the bottom of the 2 x 10 scrap. Then measure from the outside edge of the sill to the wall. Mark the dimensions on both brackets and cut with a backsaw.

4. Attach the brackets to the wall by screws through the exterior siding and into the studs of the wall frame. If you position the brackets just to the outside of the window, you should strike a stud. Use galvanized wood screws that are 1½ inches thicker than the bracket to attach them to the wall. Predrill the holes. Attach the brackets so that the top of the 2 x 10 will be approximately ⅛ inch below the top of the windowsill. Washers will be placed on top of the bracket to bring the edge of the 2 x 10 flush with the windowsill and to provide a slight slope so that water will drain toward the drainage holes.

Positioning the Shelf

5. After the brackets are attached, position the shelf on top of them. Check to make sure that the shelf is just below the top of the sill. If it isn't, adjust the brackets. On the end of the bracket closest to the wall, place a couple of washers between the bracket and the shelf so that the edge of the shelf is flush with the edge of the sill. This causes the outside edge of the shelf to tilt slightly.

6. Attach the brackets to the shelf with galvanized wood screws that are 1 inch longer than the thickness of the bracket. For added strength, toenail the shelf to the sill by angling screws through the bottom of the shelf into the sill (see the **illustration**).

Finishing

7. Caulk the seam where the 1 x 3 and quarter round are attached to the 2 x 10. *Do not* caulk the seam where the shelf joins the sill.

8. Use a nail set to countersink all the nails in the 1 x 3 and the quarter round. Fill the holes with wood filler and then sand them smooth when the filler is dry. Paint the shelf and the brackets the same color as the window trim. (Use an exterior oil-based primer and follow with exterior latex paint.) Mix a mildew retardant into the paint, since the area will be exposed to a lot of moisture.

Window Box

A window box lends beauty to the wall even before it is filled with colorful flowers.

Window boxes have been used for centuries to add natural color and interest to houses. Because a window box can be planted to reflect the changing seasons, it allows you to enjoy annual flowers, tender foliage plants, or holiday displays. In the summer, you can fill this window box with impatiens, ferns, and a trailing vine, such as variegated periwinkle. Another great summer choice is scarlet sage for attracting hummingbirds. In the winter try planting cheerful pansies, variegated ivy, and ornamental cabbage. During the holidays fill the box with greenery and ribbons. A window box also makes a wonderful miniature herb garden, with plants such as chives, parsley, and mint.

This window box is easy to make, is sturdier than many store-bought versions, and has a classic design that suits many houses. For a contemporary look, leave off the beauty molding. Use a naturally

WOOD

Pieces	Quantity	Size	Length	Notes
Ends/Brackets	2	2 x 10	18"	Cut curves.
Front	1	1 x 10	To match window	
Back	1	1 x 10	3" less than front	
Bottom	1	1 x 10	Same as back	Rip to 7¾".
Spacer blocks	2 or 3	1 x 2		
Beauty molding	1	1"	8' for 40" box	Cut to fit; miter corners.
Brackets	4	2 x 2	15"	May be cut longer if desired.

OTHER MATERIALS

4-penny galvanized nails	Exterior oil-based primer
8-penny galvanized casing nails	Exterior latex paint
¼" x 3½" lag bolts	Sandpaper
Wood filler	Metal brackets (optional)

TOOLS

Circular saw

Drill with appropriate bits

18" flexible curve (available at drafting and art supply stores)

Hammer

Nail set

Saber saw or band saw

Square

Tape measure

Wrench

handsome, rot-resistant wood, such as redwood or pressure-treated pine, and do not paint the box.

When deciding where to put your window box, remember that it is a shallow container garden that will require regular—perhaps daily—watering in the summer. Feed plants with a liquid fertilizer solution once a week.

Getting Started

The window box should be constructed from rot-resistant material, such as pressure-treated pine, heartwood cedar, or redwood. If you are using cedar or redwood, place a plastic liner (with drainage holes in the bottom) inside the box to hold the potting soil and the plants. If you can't find a liner to fit your box, have a metal one custom-made at a heating and air-conditioning shop. You can even fashion a temporary liner out of black plastic bags—which will only last a year—with holes poked in the bottom.

The ends of the box are cut from 2 x 10 material; the front and the back are cut from 1 x 10s. The back is recessed to create a ¾-inch gap between the back of the box and the wall of the house. The bottom of the box is made from 1 x 10 material ripped to 7¾ inches. Drainage holes are drilled in the bottom to allow water to flow out freely.

Construction

1. Determine how long the window box should be to fit under the chosen window. This measurement will be the length needed for the front 1 x 10. The length of the back 1 x 10 will be 3 inches less.

Cutting the Pieces

2. Cut the front and back pieces. Next, cut two pieces of 2 x 10, each 18 inches long. These will be the end pieces, which also serve as brackets. On one of the pieces, measure down the edge and mark at 9½ inches. This is where the front 1 x 10 ends and the curve of the bracket begins. Use an 18-inch flexible curve to lay out the curves on the piece. When you are satisfied with the curves, cut out the piece with a saber saw or a band saw. Then mark and cut the second piece, using the first as a pattern.

Assembling the Box

3. Attach the front 1 x 10 piece to the two end/bracket pieces with 8-penny galvanized casing nails. Make sure the edges are flush at the top and on the ends.

4. Prepare the back 1 x 10 to be attached to the rear of the end/bracket pieces. First, attach 1 x 2 spacer blocks to one side of the back. Use 4-penny galvanized nails to attach the blocks where they will line up with the 2 x 4 studs below the window in the wall frame of the house. (You may have to do a bit of detective work to locate the studs below the window. A magnetic stud finder, available at hardware stores, may help you locate them.) When you locate a stud, measure over 16 inches in either direction to locate another. Attach as many 1 x 2 spacer blocks as there are studs below the window.

5. After the blocks are attached, drill a ¼-inch hole through the block and the back piece. Make these pilot holes about 3 inches from the top edge of the back piece. Use lag bolts screwed through the holes to secure the box to the wall of the house.

OVERVIEW OF THE BOX

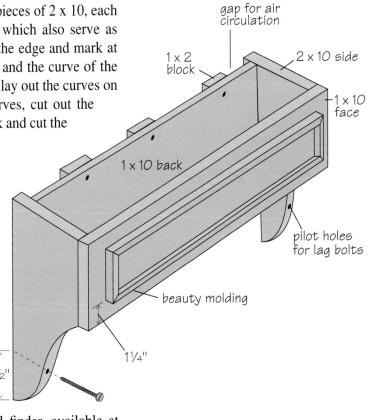

gap for air circulation

1 x 2 block

2 x 10 side

1 x 10 face

1 x 10 back

pilot holes for lag bolts

beauty molding

1¼"

2½"

111

TIPS FOR SUCCESS

❖

- If you use pressure-treated Southern pine, build the box first; then let the wood season for approximately two weeks before priming and painting. This prevents excessive warping.

- If you don't have a flexible curve to help you make the curves for the end/bracket pieces, draw a curve freehand on a 9¼- x 18-inch piece of paper. When you are satisfied with the curve, cut it out with scissors and trace the outline onto one of the 2 x 10 pieces. Cut the curve from the 2 x 10 and then use that piece as a pattern for the remaining piece.

6. Attach the prepared back to the end/bracket pieces. For easy alignment, place the back on a level work surface with the 1 x 2 spacers down. Position the end/bracket and front-piece assembly over the back. Set the top edges of the back piece flush with the two end/bracket pieces, using 8-penny galvanized casing nails to secure the back to the end pieces.

Installing the Base

7. The next step is to install the bottom of the box. First, cut a 1 x 10 to the same length as the back piece. Then rip it to the width of the opening in the bottom of the box. Place the bottom piece in the box, aligning it flush with the bottom edges of the front and back pieces. Nail the bottom piece as you did the other pieces. To provide drainage, drill two rows of ½-inch holes, spacing the holes 5 inches apart and the rows approximately 3 inches apart.

8. Dress up your new window box by attaching a rectangle of beauty molding to the front. Cut the molding so that it can be attached 1¼ inches inside the edges of the front piece. Miter the corners and attach the pieces with 4-penny galvanized finishing nails.

Finishing

9. Use a nail set to countersink all the nails. Plug the holes with wood filler and sand the filler smooth when dry. Apply a coat of exterior oil-based primer to all the surfaces, including the inside of the box, and let it dry thoroughly. Then use a quality exterior latex paint to paint the box to match the window trim.

Installing the Box

10. After the paint has dried, install your new window box. Position it and then screw ¼-inch lag bolts through the holes near the top of the back piece. Use bolts that are 3½ inches long. Drill a ¼-inch hole near the bottom of each end/bracket. Countersink the hole made by the bolt head so that it will not be so obvious. Use the same size lag bolts to secure these pieces to the wall (see the **illustration** on page 111).

Touch up any paint that was smudged during the installation. Fill the box with potting soil and your favorite plants.

Planter Box

A wooden planter freshens up a deck or a patio.

A planter filled with colorful flowers can add a cheerful note to almost any setting. Elegant wooden planters can be pricey, but you can make one in a day if you have some basic woodworking tools and skills. This planter is custom-built to hold an inexpensive plastic liner, available at garden centers and hardware or discount stores. The liner makes it possible to vary seasonal flowers, herbs, or even small vegetables for year-round appeal. The lightweight planter is easy to move, so you can accommodate sun- or shade-loving plants. The box is built of readily available materials, and the design can be altered to suit your degree of woodworking expertise and the tools at your disposal.

WOOD

Pieces	Quantity	Thickness	Size	Notes
Sides	2	¾"	5½" x 29⅞"	Adjust length to fit.
Ends	2	¾"	5½" x 6⅞"	Adjust length to fit.
Bottom supports	3	¾"	1½" x 6⅞"	Cut from 1 x 2 to fit.
Base sides	2	¾"	3½" x 31⅜"	Miter ends.
Base ends	2	¾"	3½" x 9⅞"	Miter ends.
Top trim	2	¾"	1½" x 31⅜"	Miter ends.
Top trim	2	¾"	1½" x 9⅞"	Miter ends.
Molding	1	¾"	1½" x 8'	Cut to fit.

Note: All sizes are actual. Sides and ends are cut from 1 x 6s (¾" x 5½" actual). Bottom support and top trim are cut from 1 x 2 strips (¾" x 1½" actual); base sides and ends are cut from 1 x 4 boards (¾" x 3½" actual). These dimensions accommodate a plastic liner approximately 6⅝" x 28⅛". Adjust dimensions to fit other-sized planters.

TOOLS

Backsaw

Band saw, saber saw, or coping saw

Compass or large disc for tracing arcs

Drill with appropriate bits

Hammer

Miter box

Nail set

Paintbrush

Router with roman ogee bit or hand plane

Ruler

Sanding block and sandpaper

Square

Straight edge

OTHER MATERIALS

Plastic liner

4-penny galvanized finishing nails

6-penny galvanized finishing nails

Exterior waterproof wood glue

Wood filler

Exterior oil-based primer (optional)

Exterior latex paint or stain

Getting Started

First, purchase the plastic liner. Buy a sturdy liner similar to the one pictured on page 117. The liner will determine the size of the main box. Once you know the liner's dimensions, building the planter box is a bit like wrapping a package. (Dimensions for the liner used here are 6⅝ inches wide x 28⅛ inches long and about 4¾ inches deep.)

The planter box itself consists of five components: the main box, the bottom supports, the base, the top trim, and the decorative molding. The main box is built first. Then the bottom supports are installed to hold the weight of the plastic liner. Next, a base is nailed to the main box to serve as the legs of the planter. The top trim is attached to the top of the main box to hide the lip of the plastic liner

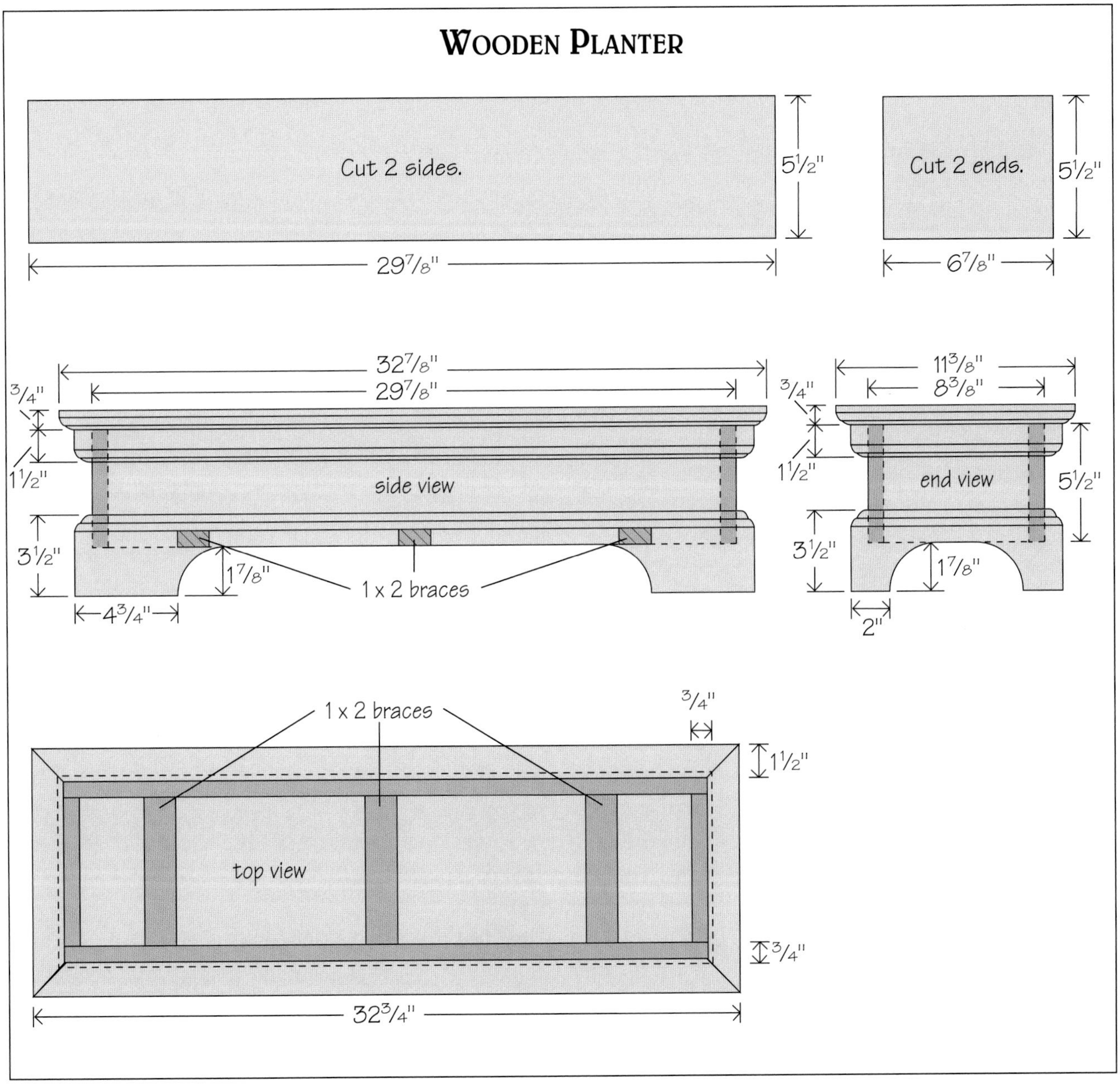
WOODEN PLANTER
Cut 2 sides.
5½"
29⅞"
Cut 2 ends.
5½"
6⅞"
32⅞"
29⅞"
¾"
1½"
side view
3½"
1⅞"
1 x 2 braces
4¾"
11⅜"
8⅜"
¾"
1½"
end view
5½"
3½"
1⅞"
2"
1 x 2 braces
¾"
1½"
top view
¾"
32¾"

and to aesthetically balance the top and the bottom. The decorative molding gives the planter box a finished look.

Construction

1. Carefully measure the outside width and length of the plastic liner. Since the sides are tapered, be sure to measure at the top, where the

TIPS FOR SUCCESS
———— ❖ ————

• Use rot-resistant or pressure-treated wood for a planter that will last a long time.

• Apply exterior waterproof wood glue (such as Titebond II) with a small disposable brush to surfaces that will be nailed together. This will help prevent warping from weather and plant watering.

dimensions are the greatest. For the sides of the main box, cut two pieces of 1 x 6 to 1¾ inches longer than the length of the liner (1½ inches extra because the sides will cover the two ¾-inch-wide end pieces and an extra ¼ inch to allow an ⅛-inch clearance on each end of the liner).

2. Cut two end pieces ¼ inch longer than the width measurement to produce an ⅛-inch clearance on each side of the liner. Nail the side pieces onto the end pieces, using 6-penny galvanized finishing nails and exterior wood glue. Predrill these and all other nail holes to avoid splitting the wood.

Bottom Supports

3. Cut and install the 1 x 2 bottom supports. Their length should be exactly the width of the inside of the bottom of the main box. Determine the position of the supports by slipping the plastic liner into the main box.

4. Turn the box and the plastic liner upside down on the workbench. Fit the supports into the box so that they rest on the bottom of the liner, spacing them equally along the length. Nail through the sides of the main box and into the supports, using 6-penny galvanized finishing nails.

Base

5. Next comes the base. Start with a piece of 1 x 4 about 10 inches longer than the combined length of both side pieces and both end pieces of the main box. If you have a router, fit it with a roman ogee bit and rout one edge. If you do not have a router, soften the corner with a hand plane or sandpaper or both.

6. Cut the prepared board to fit snugly around the main box. Miter for a professional-looking job. Once you have the four pieces cut to length, mark the arcs that will be cut out. If you don't have a suitable compass for drawing the arcs, check around the kitchen for something circular with an appropriate diameter; a coffee can, a saucer, or a plate should work just fine. Trace the arcs onto the base pieces (shown in the **illustration** on page 115). Cut out the arcs using a band saw, a saber saw, or a coping saw. Smooth any irregularities with sandpaper. Attach the base pieces to the main box so that the bottom edge of the main box is flush with or just slightly above the cutouts. Use 4-penny galvanized finishing nails to attach the base to the main box.

Top Trim

7. Use a 1 x 2 to make the top trim. Prepare the edge with the router or with a plane and sandpaper as you did with the base piece. Carefully measure and miter the pieces so that they fit snugly around the top of the main box. Position the prepared edge down so that it complements the prepared edge of the base. Use 4-penny nails to attach the trim to the main box. The trim should be higher than the edge of the main box so that it will hide the lip of the plastic liner. Place the plastic liner inside the main box to determine the position of the trim.

Decorative Molding

8. The decorative molding is cut from a length of molding purchased from a home-supply store. Miter the ends and attach the molding to the top edge of the trim. Use 4-penny nails or, if you prefer, use exterior wood glue to avoid making nail holes.

Finishing

9. Countersink all nails with a nail set and fill the holes with a quality wood filler. If your miters do not match just right, wood filler can help there, too. Once the filler has dried, sand it smooth. Also sand any other irregularities. Prime with a quality exterior oil-based primer and paint with exterior latex paint. If using treated wood that has not been kiln-dried after treating, let the planter season a couple of months before finishing. The planter may also be stained instead of painted.

Miter the base, top trim, and decorative molding pieces for a professional look.

The plants in the planter's plastic liner can be changed easily, assuring a spot of color regardless of the season.

Mailbox

A customized mailbox is more than a receptacle for mail: it's an artistic statement.

TOOLS

Circular saw

Drill with appropriate bits

Scissors

Screwdriver

Sponges

Square

Wrench

MATERIALS

Cedar or pressure-treated mail-box post, unassembled

White mailbox

Decorative bracket

Wood finial

White gloss exterior latex paint

Green exterior enamel paint

Oil-based exterior primer

8" metal corner brace

1" galvanized wood screws

1½" galvanized wood screws

¼" x 3½" lag bolts

Wood filler

Sandpaper

For many people, mailboxes don't just hold the mail—they serve as a canvas for the homeowner's creativity. This mailbox began as a ready-to-assemble product from a home-supply store. With an ivy-shaped cutout sponge, some paint, and the addition of a finial and a decorative bracket, it became a charming yard addition. You can use the same sponge-painting technique with different colors of paint to decorate a mailbox with other distinctively shaped leaves, such as maple or ginkgo, or easy geometric shapes, such as a star or a moon. A decorative mailbox can even be used as a feature elsewhere in the yard: it is a convenient place to store gloves and small garden tools.

Getting Started

You can improve the ready-to-assemble wooden mailbox posts found at most home-supply stores by shortening the post and by adding a finial to the top. Discard the chunky support piece and use instead an inconspicuous 8-inch corner brace to provide the needed support.

Sponge-painting with cutout ivy leaves is a quick-and-easy method of adding interest to an ordinary white mailbox.

Assembling the Post

1. Purchase a ready-to-assemble wooden mailbox post at your local home-supply store. Lay the post on the ground with the arm in place. Position the mailbox on the arm and measure 5 inches from the top of the mailbox. Using a pencil and a square, draw a line (see the **box** at right). Continue the line around the post at that point and cut the post with a circular saw. Drill a hole in the center of the top end of the post and insert the finial.

2. Don't bother to attach the support piece that comes with the post. Instead, install an 8-inch metal corner brace to help support the arm. Using 1-inch galvanized wood screws, attach the brace to the front side of the post and on the top side of the arm. The mailbox will hide the brace, and the underside of the arm will be available for attachment of a decorative piece.

TIP FOR SUCCESS

To find the center of the post to drill a hole for the finial, draw one line each to connect opposite corners of the post. The lines intersect in the center.

READY-TO-ASSEMBLE PIECES

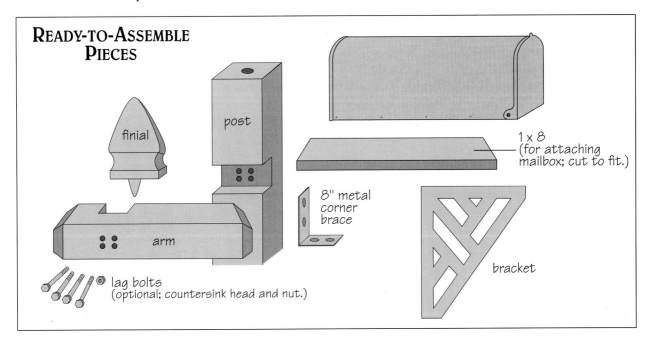

finial

post

arm

lag bolts
(optional; countersink head and nut.)

8" metal corner brace

1 x 8
(for attaching mailbox; cut to fit.)

bracket

USING FRESH LEAVES

When collecting ivy leaves, pick a whole sprig to use as a positioning guide. Leaves should face each other at the base, with the tips pointing outward at various angles.

Make several leaf-shaped sponges by tracing around leaves of varying sizes. Practice stamping on paper first; then use the two or three best sponges to decorate the mailbox.

Don't paint leaves in the area that will be covered by the flag when it's down. Preserving the white space keeps the pattern looking neat.

Supporting the Arm

3. For added support for the arm, use lag bolts to attach the arm to the post. Use a ¼-inch bit to drill four holes in the arm where it will attach to the post (also drill countersink holes). Put the arm in place and use a smaller bit to drill four pilot holes about 1 inch deep in the post. Screw in four ¼-inch lag bolts that are 3½ inches long (see the **illustration** on page 119). Countersink the heads and plug the holes with wood filler. Sand the filler when it is dry. After you paint the posts, no one but you will know that the lag bolts are there.

Placing the Mailbox

4. Cut a 1 x 8 to fit inside the bottom of the mailbox and attach it to the arm with three 1½-inch galvanized wood screws. Make sure there is enough room between the back of the board and the post to slip the mailbox over the 1 x 8 board.

5. Use a prefabricated decorative bracket, available from lumberyards and catalogs, to trim the underside of the arm. Attach the bracket to the arm and to the post with 1½-inch galvanized wood screws.

Finishing

6. Prime the entire post with an oil-based exterior primer. Then give it two coats of glossy white exterior latex. Using just one color on the post, the arm, the bracket, and the finial makes everything look as if it were made to go together.

7. The final step is to finish the mailbox itself by cutting several ivy-leaf patterns and then sponge-painting across the top and along the edges.

　　Make the cutouts. Trace an ivy leaf on a flat, dry sponge. Cut out the shape with a pair of scissors. Repeat for a variety of sizes of leaf cutouts.

　　Stamp the mailbox. Thoroughly wet a cutout and then squeeze it to remove the excess water. Dip the cutout into the green exterior enamel paint. Blot it once on a paper towel to prevent dripping and then press the cutout against the mailbox where desired. Make sure that the entire surface of the cutout comes in contact with the mailbox. Press harder around the edges than in the center of the cutout to get a more textured appearance. Stamp leaves along the edge and up over the top of the mailbox, using a variety of cutout sizes. Add a few leaves to the door for a finishing touch.

Do You Know?

Safety Tips

Safety should be the primary concern of all gardeners—all the time. Laboring in the elements with ordinary gardening tools presents several situations in which safety may be compromised easily. Working with power tools and sharp hand tools sets up even more potentially dangerous situations.

By following the simple safety rules below, you can greatly minimize the inherent risks associated with the various tools needed to carry out the projects in this book.

- When driving nails or operating any type of power equipment, always wear protective eyewear.

- If operating a tool or any equipment that is very loud (such as a chain saw) or that produces a high-pitched noise (such as a router), be sure to wear ear protection.

- Always read the owner's manual for any power tool that you plan to use and understand fully how to operate the tool before proceeding.

- When handling pressure-treated wood, always wear gloves, eye protection, and a dust mask. (But *never* wear gloves when operating a power woodworking tool, such as a saw, a drill, a planer, or a sander.)

- Make sure that the lighting and the ventilation in your work area are adequate.

- Only use extension cords that are properly rated for the task you have in mind.

- When working in hot weather, drink plenty of liquids to stay completely hydrated. Know the signs of heat-stroke and take precautions.

- If working in extremely cold weather, dress appropriately and avoid frostbite or any dangers from exposure.

Wood

Here are a few important things about wood and lumber that can make your woodworking projects more successful.

Lumber Dimensions

For someone unfamiliar with lumber dimensions, it can be frustrating to be directed to allow 1½ inches for the thickness of a 2 x 4. Why wouldn't a 2 x 4 be 2 inches thick? But not only is it not 2 inches thick, it's also not 4 inches wide. In fact, none of the terms used to refer to common sizes of lumber accurately reflect their dimensions.

Just what *are* the actual dimensions? In general, a board with 2 by any number (2 x 2, 2 x 4, 2 x 6) is 1½ inches thick and ½ inch less in width than the name implies. This is true for lumber up to 8 inches in width. Material listed as 8 inches or greater is ¾ inch less in width than the name implies. For example, a 2 x 6 is 1½ inches thick by 5½ inches wide, a 2 x 8 is 1½ inches thick by 7¼ inches wide, a 2 x 10 is 1½ inches thick by 9¼ inches wide, and a 2 x 12 is 1½ inches thick by 11¼ inches wide.

Material referred to as 1 by any number follows the same rules for width. Actual thickness is ¾ inch.

Lengths of lumber are more straightforward. Lumber is usually sold in lengths of 8 feet (and these are actual), with increases in increments of 2 feet.

Much of the lumber used for the projects in this book is pressure-treated pine. This is ordinary pinewood that has been impregnated with chemicals to retard or to prevent the wood from rotting or from being attacked by insects. The amount of chemical forced into the structure of the wood is used as a basis for determining the appropriate use of the wood. If you plan to build something that will place the pressure-treated wood in direct contact with the ground, this lumber should be tagged or marked as rated for ground contact or should have a retention level number of 0.40 or higher.

Nails

Different nails serve different purposes. Here is a quick look at some of the kinds of nails called for to complete the projects in this book.

The size of the nail is designated by a number. The larger the number, the bigger (in both length and diameter) the nail. If a particular kind of nail is called for, a description of the function will be included in the name. An 8-penny finishing nail is the size of an ordinary 8-penny nail but has a much smaller head, which can be easily countersunk. A 16-penny casing nail is the size of an ordinary 16-penny nail, but it, too, has a smaller head that is easily countersunk.

Many of the projects in this book call for galvanized nails. These nails are covered with a galvanized coating that helps them stand up to weather conditions for a much longer time than an ordinary nail. In general, if a nail or a screw will be exposed to the elements, it should be galvanized.

Garden Tools Guide

The implements required for carrying out the projects in this book generally are commonly owned garden tools. If you don't have them all or need to replace one, here are some guidelines for selecting the right tool.

Bow rake. This is ideal for smoothing soil for planting vegetables, flowers, or grass seed. It pulls out stone, weeds, and clods of soil and is also good for mixing in

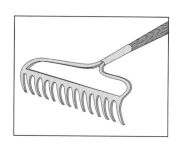

fertilizer and for leveling planting beds. The rake's tines and bow should be forged from one piece of steel rather than welded together.

Garden cart. Since it has two wheels, a garden cart is more stable than the most sturdy wheelbarrow. Its disadvantage is that it is not as easily maneuvered between garden rows and around shrubs and between tight spots. Garden carts come in two basic styles. The lawn (or leaf) cart is like a deep bucket, usually with the front side tilted at a 45-degree angle. This allows the front to lay flat on the ground when the cart is tilted forward, making it easy to rake leaves into it. However,

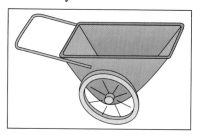

lawn cart

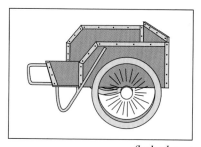

flatbed cart

this design also makes it a bit difficult to shovel material out. The other garden cart style is more like a flatbed wagon. It is ideal for hauling bales of pine straw or other big loads, and it is easy to shovel from the bed. In either style, look for a sturdy, noncorrosive frame, with large wheels and air-filled tires.

Hoe. This tool is used for making hills and rows in a vegetable garden, for leveling soil, for preparing spots

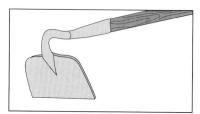

for reseeding or sodding, and for weeding. In the best hoes, the blade and the shank are forged from one piece of steel. Look for a strong wooden handle.

Leaf rake. Buy a sturdy model that feels comfortable to you. The tines should be hefty enough to stand up to the demands of raking leaves, grass clippings, mulch, and debris. A reinforcement bar across the tines helps keep them from bending.

Loppers. These are a larger variation of pruners and are designed to cut much larger branches. Look for a scissors type. Since they are operated with both hands, loppers are easily opened for each cut. The long handles afford a great deal of leverage, so look for loppers with strong handles that won't be broken easily.

Pruners. These handheld cutters are used for pruning small branches and flowers. For a cleaner cut, buy a scissors type not an anvil type. Spring-loaded pruners that open on their own after each cut save you time.

Round-point shovel. Used for all kinds of general digging jobs, this is one tool that is absolutely required. Look for a shovel with a long, smooth wooden handle and a closed back where the handle comes down into the

blade, as dirt can collect in an open groove in the back, causing the handle to rot. Also, the top edge of the shovel (where you put your foot to help push the tool into the ground) should be rolled over slightly.

Trowel. There are two types of trowels. A garden trowel is very handy for planting or for digging up small garden plants. It can also be useful when fine-tuning an excavation job, such as for setting the edging material for a walkway. A good trowel has a one-piece blade and a shank and a wooden handle. Masonry trowels, used in working with concrete and brick, come

in a variety of sizes and shapes, depending on the specific use for which it is intended. Seek advice at a hardware store or from an experienced mason as to the best masonry trowel needed for your project.

Wheelbarrow. There are many different models and types of wheelbarrows from which to choose, depending on the use. For general hauling of dirt, plants, pine straw, compost, brick, firewood, and such, buy a contractor's wheelbarrow. It has a deep tray, and its sturdy undercarriage makes it stable. Its long wooden handles extend all the way to the wheel for good leverage. If the classic contractor's wheelbarrow is too heavy for you, consider getting a smaller one with a polyethylene tray. This wheelbarrow is lighter and produces less noise

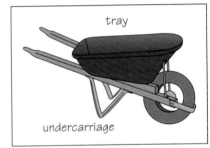

contractor's wheelbarrow

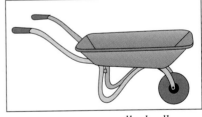

small wheelbarrow

when you drop something into it. Don't forget to inspect the tire. The best kind is a pneumatic tire, which is filled with air.

Glossary

Backfill: *(n)* Material used to fill in around new structures, such as walls and terraces, so that the level around the structure equals the level of the surrounding ground. *(v)* To place backfill material.

Biscuit joiner: *(n)* A handheld electric power tool used in preparing wooden boards that are to be joined. The biscuit joiner cuts a small slot in the edge of the boards. A wooden "biscuit," shaped to fit the slot, is then glued in the slots, giving strength to the joint.

Branch collar: *(n)* The swollen area of the tree trunk where the branch joins the trunk.

Broad-bladed cold chisel: *(n)* A metal tool with a broad, sharp, beveled edge, used in conjunction with a hammer or a mallet to cut stone or brick.

Butt joint: *(n)* A joint in which the end or the edge of one board is set squarely against the face or the edge of another.

Caulk: *(n)* A pliable material used to fill in gaps in seams where two or more boards or panels meet. *(v)* To apply caulk.

Chamfer: *(n)* A slightly beveled or rounded edge or corner. *(v)* To slightly bevel or to round an edge or a corner.

Checking: *(n)* A lumber defect in which splits develop lengthwise across the growth rings of wood.

Cleat: *(n)* A strip of wood used to give strength or support.

Concrete joint tool: *(n)* A metal hand tool used to smooth or to shape concrete joints or edges.

Coping saw: *(n)* A small handsaw with a very narrow blade held in a steel bow frame. It is used for cutting curves.

Countersink: *(v)* To recess a nail or screw head so that it will be hidden. In general, a nail is countersunk using a nail set to drive the nail head below the surface of the wood, and a screw is countersunk by enlarging the surface end of the screw hole so that the screw head can be recessed below the surface of the board.

Course: *(n)* A continuous layer of building material, such as brick, stone, tile, or shingles, on a wall or on a roof.

Dado: *(n)* A rectangular channel cut across the grain of a board in preparation for joining two boards.

Dado blade: *(n)* A special saw blade for a table saw or a radial arm saw, designed for making dadoes.

Dovetail: *(n)* A fan-shaped pattern cut into a piece of wood that forms a tight interlocking joint when fitted into a corresponding cutout in another piece of wood.

Dovetail joint: *(n)* A strong, attractive woodworking joint that utilizes dovetails.

Garden fork: *(n)* A large fork that has a strong handle and is used for turning soil, compost, and other materials.

Lap joint: *(n)* A joint in which matching dadoes overlap to join two boards.

Lath strip: *(n)* A narrow, thin piece of wood.

Mattock: *(n)* A hand-digging tool with a short handle and a blade set at right angles to the handle.

Miter: *(v)* To cut the end of a board at a 45-degree angle so that when the board is joined to another board cut in a similar manner, the two boards form a 90-degree angle.

Mortar joint tool: *(n)* A metal hand tool used to smooth the mortar in the joints between brick, concrete blocks, or stone.

Nail set: *(n)* A small metal handheld tool used in conjunction with a hammer to countersink nails.

Nonaggregate concrete mix: *(n)* Prepackaged concrete mix that contains no gravel (aggregate).

Pilot hole: *(n)* A small hole drilled into a piece of wood where a wood screw or a lag bolt will be inserted. The hole is smaller in diameter and slightly shorter in length than the screw or the bolt.

Quarter round: *(n)* A type of molding that takes its name from its shape. It is essentially a round dowel that has been cut lengthwise (ripped) into quarters.

Rebar: *(n)* Short for reinforcing bar, this steel bar is used to reinforce concrete structures. Also used as stakes to drive into hard ground.

Rip: *(v)* To saw a board lengthwise.

Roman ogee bit: *(n)* A router bit used to cut a decorative edge with an S-shaped profile.

Rout: *(v)* To cut away a portion of a board with a router.

Router: *(n)* A portable electric tool used in woodworking to make grooves, decorative edges, and special cuts for joining wood.

Rubble: *(n)* Irregularly shaped, quarried stone that are too small or irregular to be entered into a higher category by the stone supplier.

Screed: *(n)* A long, straight board used for leveling and removing excess concrete, sand, or other materials.

Shim: *(n)* A thin piece of material used as a leveler or as a spacer. *(v)* To level or to adjust by using a shim.

Square: *(n)* A carpentry tool used for checking or for marking 90-degree angles.

Tamp: *(n)* A tool or an instrument used to compact with a series of blows or taps. *(v)* To compact with a series of blows or taps.

Toenail: *(v)* To secure a board or a beam by driving a nail at an angle through one board and into another, to which the first board is being attached.

U-channel strip: *(n)* Lumber that has a prerouted U-shaped groove centered on one side. It is used for making frames for lattice panels or other panel materials, such as plywood.

Uplight: *(n)* A theatrical term referring to one of the lights at the front of a stage that shines up from the floor.

Wire brad: *(n)* A very small nail with a slight side projection instead of a head.

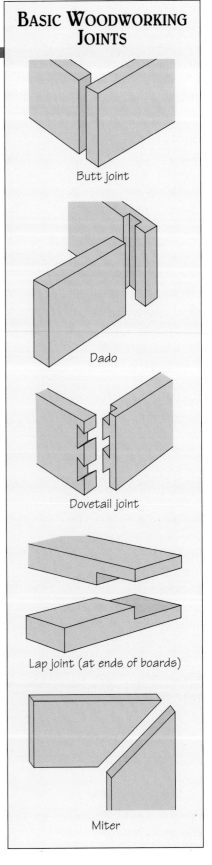

BASIC WOODWORKING JOINTS

Butt joint

Dado

Dovetail joint

Lap joint (at ends of boards)

Miter

Index

Index

Special Thanks

Louis Joyner, Building Editor,
    Southern Living magazine
Julia Hamilton Thomason,
    Homes Editor, *Southern
    Living* magazine
Van Chaplin
Jennifer Greer
Charlotte Hagood
Cathy Ritter
Southern Progress Corporation
    Library Staff